This Book Belongs To:

Contact Information	
Name:	
Address:	
Phone:	

Start / End Dates

/ / to / /

Dedication

This book is dedicated to all the meditators around the world, who practice meditation and get in touch with the breath which connects us all!

You are my inspiration for producing books and I'm excited to help in reflecting on your meditation practice – and make the world more centered and accepting!

How To Use This Meditation Journal

The purpose of this Meditation Reflection Notebook is for anyone to reflect on their meditation practice while holding themselves accountable to meditate on a regular basis.

Here are some simple guidelines to follow so you can make the most of this book:

1. The first section is to record the Date, Time, Location, Duration, Method, and Mantra of your meditation, to keep you on track and accountable.
2. As you progress in your practice, you may find recording your body position useful in the "Meditation Position" section.
3. Setting an intention for your meditation can be an important aspect of manifesting the kind of life you want. That's where the "Meditation Focus" section can help out.
4. The "Mood Wheel" section is helpful for tracking your mood before you meditate – from Happy, Sad, Disgust, Anger, Fear to Surprise, use this section to see how your meditation is helping.
5. Writing down your thoughts in the "Thoughts and Insights" section will help you process your thoughts and dig out insights from your practice.
6. Not every day meditating will feel the same. With the "Quality and Intensity" section, you can see how all the other sections affect the quality and intensity of your practice – and start to see yourself from a healthy perspective as you gain distance from your thinking mind.
7. Lastly, the "Reflections" section sets you up to feel grateful, accomplished, and clear about what you can work on. It really ties everything together to help you feel progress in your meditation practice and life.

Enjoy the journey!

📅 DATE	🕐 TIME
📍 LOCATION	⏱️ DURATION
🧘 METHOD	❊ MANTRA

MEDITATION POSITION

🧘	🪑	🧍	🛌	🤸
☐	☐	☐	☐	☐

MEDITATION FOCUS

MOOD WHEEL

Mood wheel with inner emotions: HAPPY, SAD, SURPRISE, DISGUST, FEAR, ANGER
Middle ring: OPTIMISTIC, PROUD, GUILTY, DEPRESSED, PEACEFUL, LONELY, CONFUSED, DISAPPROVAL, EXCITED, AWFUL, AMAZED, DISAPPOINTED, INSECURE, AGGRESSIVE, HUMILIATED, MAD, SCARED, HURT

THOUGHTS & INSIGHTS

QUALITY AND INTENSITY

FOCUS AND BREATHING — 1 — 2 — 3 — 4 — 5 — 6 — 7 — 8 — 9 — 10

VISIONS AND EMOTIONS

REFLECTIONS

🙏 I am grateful for ...

⛰️ I will accomplish ...

📈 I need to work on ...

	DATE		TIME
	LOCATION		DURATION
	METHOD		MANTRA

MEDITATION POSITION

☐ ☐ ☐ ☐ ☐

MEDITATION FOCUS

MOOD WHEEL

Mood wheel emotions: HAPPY, SAD, DISGUST, ANGER, FEAR, SURPRISE — OPTIMISTIC, PROUD, GUILTY, DEPRESSED, LONELY, DISAPPROVAL, AWFUL, DISAPPOINTED, AGGRESSIVE, MAD, HURT, SCARED, HUMILIATED, INSECURE, AMAZED, EXCITED, CONFUSED, PEACEFUL

THOUGHTS & INSIGHTS

QUALITY AND INTENSITY

FOCUS AND BREATHING — 1 — 2 — 3 — 4 — 5 — 6 — 7 — 8 — 9 — 10

VISIONS AND EMOTIONS

REFLECTIONS

I am grateful for …

I will accomplish …

I need to work on …

📅 DATE	🕐 TIME
📍 LOCATION	⏱️ DURATION
🧘 METHOD	🌸 MANTRA

MEDITATION POSITION

☐   ☐   ☐   ☐   ☐

MEDITATION FOCUS

MOOD WHEEL

Inner ring: HAPPY, SAD, DISGUST, ANGER, FEAR, SURPRISE

Middle ring: OPTIMISTIC, PROUD, GUILTY, DEPRESSED, LONELY, DISAPPROVAL, AWFUL, DISAPPOINTED, AGGRESSIVE, MAD, HURT, SCARED, HUMILIATED, INSECURE, AMAZED, EXCITED, CONFUSED, PEACEFUL

THOUGHTS & INSIGHTS

QUALITY AND INTENSITY

FOCUS AND BREATHING — 1 — 2 — 3 — 4 — 5 — 6 — 7 — 8 — 9 — 10

VISIONS AND EMOTIONS — 1 — 2 — 3 — 4 — 5 — 6 — 7 — 8 — 9 — 10

REFLECTIONS

🙏 I am grateful for ...

⛰️ I will accomplish ...

⚙️ I need to work on ...

📅 DATE	🕐 TIME
📍 LOCATION	⏱️ DURATION
🧘 METHOD	❋ MANTRA

MEDITATION POSITION

☐ ☐ ☐ ☐ ☐

MEDITATION FOCUS

MOOD WHEEL

Mood wheel with emotions: OPTIMISTIC, PROUD, GUILTY, DEPRESSED, PEACEFUL, LONELY, CONFUSED, DISAPPROVAL, EXCITED, AWFUL, AMAZED, DISAPPOINTED, INSECURE, AGGRESSIVE, HUMILIATED, MAD, SCARED, HURT — inner ring: HAPPY, SAD, SURPRISE, DISGUST, FEAR, ANGER

THOUGHTS & INSIGHTS

QUALITY AND INTENSITY

FOCUS AND BREATHING — 1 — 2 — 3 — 4 — 5 — 6 — 7 — 8 — 9 — 10

VISIONS AND EMOTIONS

REFLECTIONS

🙏 I am grateful for …

⛰️ I will accomplish …

⚙️ I need to work on …

📅	DATE	🕐	TIME
📍	LOCATION	⏱️	DURATION
🧘	METHOD	✱	MANTRA

MEDITATION POSITION

🧘	🪑	🧍	🛏️	🧘‍♀️
☐	☐	☐	☐	☐

MEDITATION FOCUS

MOOD WHEEL

Mood wheel with inner emotions: HAPPY, SAD, DISGUST, ANGER, FEAR, SURPRISE
Outer emotions: OPTIMISTIC, PROUD, GUILTY, DEPRESSED, LONELY, DISAPPROVAL, AWFUL, DISAPPOINTED, AGGRESSIVE, MAD, HURT, SCARED, HUMILIATED, INSECURE, AMAZED, EXCITED, CONFUSED, PEACEFUL

THOUGHTS & INSIGHTS

QUALITY AND INTENSITY

	1	2	3	4	5	6	7	8	9	10
FOCUS AND BREATHING	○	○	○	○	○	○	○	○	○	○
VISIONS AND EMOTIONS	○	○	○	○	○	○	○	○	○	○

REFLECTIONS

🙏 I am grateful for ...

⛰️ I will accomplish ...

📊 I need to work on ...

	DATE		TIME
	LOCATION		DURATION
	METHOD		MANTRA

MEDITATION POSITION

☐ ☐ ☐ ☐ ☐

MEDITATION FOCUS

MOOD WHEEL

Mood wheel sections: HAPPY (optimistic, proud, peaceful), SAD (guilty, depressed, lonely), DISGUST (disapproval, awful, disappointed), ANGER (aggressive, mad, hurt), FEAR (scared, humiliated, insecure), SURPRISE (amazed, excited, confused)

THOUGHTS & INSIGHTS

QUALITY AND INTENSITY

FOCUS AND BREATHING — 1 — 2 — 3 — 4 — 5 — 6 — 7 — 8 — 9 — 10

VISIONS AND EMOTIONS

REFLECTIONS

I am grateful for ...

I will accomplish ...

I need to work on ...

📅 DATE	🕐 TIME
📍 LOCATION	⏱️ DURATION
🧘 METHOD	🕉️ MANTRA

MEDITATION POSITION

☐ ☐ ☐ ☐ ☐

MEDITATION FOCUS

MOOD WHEEL

Mood wheel with inner emotions: HAPPY, SAD, SURPRISE, DISGUST, FEAR, ANGER. Outer emotions: OPTIMISTIC, PROUD, GUILTY, DEPRESSED, LONELY, DISAPPROVAL, AWFUL, DISAPPOINTED, AGGRESSIVE, MAD, HURT, SCARED, HUMILIATED, INSECURE, AMAZED, EXCITED, CONFUSED, PEACEFUL.

THOUGHTS & INSIGHTS

QUALITY AND INTENSITY

FOCUS AND BREATHING — 1 — 2 — 3 — 4 — 5 — 6 — 7 — 8 — 9 — 10

VISIONS AND EMOTIONS

REFLECTIONS

🙏 I am grateful for ...

⛰️ I will accomplish ...

⚙️ I need to work on ...

DATE	TIME
LOCATION	DURATION
METHOD	MANTRA

MEDITATION POSITION

☐ ☐ ☐ ☐ ☐

MEDITATION FOCUS

MOOD WHEEL

Mood wheel with inner emotions: HAPPY, SAD, DISGUST, ANGER, FEAR, SURPRISE. Outer emotions: OPTIMISTIC, PROUD, GUILTY, DEPRESSED, PEACEFUL, LONELY, CONFUSED, DISAPPROVAL, EXCITED, AWFUL, AMAZED, DISAPPOINTED, INSECURE, AGGRESSIVE, HUMILIATED, MAD, SCARED, HURT.

THOUGHTS & INSIGHTS

QUALITY AND INTENSITY

FOCUS AND BREATHING — 1 — 2 — 3 — 4 — 5 — 6 — 7 — 8 — 9 — 10

VISIONS AND EMOTIONS

REFLECTIONS

I am grateful for ...

I will accomplish ...

I need to work on ...

📅 DATE	🕐 TIME
📍 LOCATION	⏱️ DURATION
🧘 METHOD	❄️ MANTRA

MEDITATION POSITION

🧘 ☐	🪑 ☐	🧍 ☐	🛌 ☐	🤸 ☐

MEDITATION FOCUS

MOOD WHEEL

(Mood wheel with inner ring: HAPPY, SAD, DISGUST, ANGER, FEAR, SURPRISE; outer ring: OPTIMISTIC, PROUD, GUILTY, DEPRESSED, LONELY, DISAPPROVAL, AWFUL, DISAPPOINTED, AGGRESSIVE, MAD, HURT, SCARED, HUMILIATED, INSECURE, AMAZED, EXCITED, CONFUSED, PEACEFUL)

THOUGHTS & INSIGHTS

QUALITY AND INTENSITY

FOCUS AND BREATHING ○—○—○—○—○—○—○—○—○—○
                                  1—2—3—4—5—6—7—8—9—10
VISIONS AND EMOTIONS ○—○—○—○—○—○—○—○—○—○

REFLECTIONS

👏 I am grateful for …

⛰️ I will accomplish …

📊 I need to work on …

📅 DATE	🕐 TIME
📍 LOCATION	⏱️ DURATION
🧘 METHOD	✺ MANTRA

MEDITATION POSITION

☐   ☐   ☐   ☐   ☐

MEDITATION FOCUS

MOOD WHEEL

Happy · Sad · Disgust · Anger · Fear · Surprise
Optimistic, Proud, Guilty, Depressed, Lonely, Disapproval, Awful, Disappointed, Aggressive, Mad, Hurt, Scared, Humiliated, Insecure, Amazed, Excited, Confused, Peaceful

THOUGHTS & INSIGHTS

QUALITY AND INTENSITY

FOCUS AND BREATHING — 1 — 2 — 3 — 4 — 5 — 6 — 7 — 8 — 9 — 10

VISIONS AND EMOTIONS — 1 — 2 — 3 — 4 — 5 — 6 — 7 — 8 — 9 — 10

REFLECTIONS

👏 I am grateful for …

⛰️ I will accomplish …

⚙️ I need to work on …

📅 DATE	🕐 TIME
📍 LOCATION	⏱️ DURATION
🧘 METHOD	✴️ MANTRA

MEDITATION POSITION

🧘 ☐	🪑 ☐	🧍 ☐	🛌 ☐	🤸 ☐

MEDITATION FOCUS

MOOD WHEEL

(Mood wheel with inner emotions: HAPPY, SAD, DISGUST, ANGER, FEAR, SURPRISE; outer emotions: OPTIMISTIC, PROUD, GUILTY, DEPRESSED, LONELY, DISAPPROVAL, AWFUL, DISAPPOINTED, AGGRESSIVE, MAD, HURT, SCARED, HUMILIATED, INSECURE, AMAZED, EXCITED, CONFUSED, PEACEFUL)

THOUGHTS & INSIGHTS

QUALITY AND INTENSITY

👤 FOCUS AND BREATHING	1 — 2 — 3 — 4 — 5 — 6 — 7 — 8 — 9 — 10
👁️ VISIONS AND EMOTIONS	

REFLECTIONS

🙏 I am grateful for …

⛰️ I will accomplish …

⚙️ I need to work on …

📅 DATE	🕐 TIME
📍 LOCATION	⏱️ DURATION
🧘 METHOD	❄️ MANTRA

MEDITATION POSITION

☐ ☐ ☐ ☐ ☐

MEDITATION FOCUS

MOOD WHEEL

THOUGHTS & INSIGHTS

QUALITY AND INTENSITY

FOCUS AND BREATHING — 1 — 2 — 3 — 4 — 5 — 6 — 7 — 8 — 9 — 10

VISIONS AND EMOTIONS

REFLECTIONS

I am grateful for …

I will accomplish …

I need to work on …

📅 DATE	🕐 TIME
📍 LOCATION	⏱️ DURATION
🧘 METHOD	❄️ MANTRA

MEDITATION POSITION

🧘	🪑	🧍	🛌	🤸
☐	☐	☐	☐	☐

MEDITATION FOCUS

MOOD WHEEL

Mood wheel with core emotions: HAPPY, SAD, SURPRISE, DISGUST, FEAR, ANGER; surrounded by: OPTIMISTIC, PROUD, GUILTY, DEPRESSED, PEACEFUL, LONELY, CONFUSED, DISAPPROVAL, EXCITED, AWFUL, AMAZED, DISAPPOINTED, INSECURE, AGGRESSIVE, HUMILIATED, SCARED, HURT, MAD

THOUGHTS & INSIGHTS

QUALITY AND INTENSITY

FOCUS AND BREATHING — 1 — 2 — 3 — 4 — 5 — 6 — 7 — 8 — 9 — 10

VISIONS AND EMOTIONS — 1 — 2 — 3 — 4 — 5 — 6 — 7 — 8 — 9 — 10

REFLECTIONS

🙏 I am grateful for …

⛰️ I will accomplish …

📈 I need to work on …

📅 DATE	🕐 TIME
📍 LOCATION	⏱️ DURATION
🧘 METHOD	❁ MANTRA

MEDITATION POSITION

☐ ☐ ☐ ☐ ☐

MEDITATION FOCUS

MOOD WHEEL

- HAPPY: OPTIMISTIC, PROUD, PEACEFUL
- SAD: GUILTY, DEPRESSED, LONELY
- DISGUST: DISAPPROVAL, AWFUL, DISAPPOINTED
- ANGER: AGGRESSIVE, MAD, HURT
- FEAR: SCARED, HUMILIATED, INSECURE
- SURPRISE: AMAZED, EXCITED, CONFUSED

THOUGHTS & INSIGHTS

QUALITY AND INTENSITY

FOCUS AND BREATHING — 1 — 2 — 3 — 4 — 5 — 6 — 7 — 8 — 9 — 10

VISIONS AND EMOTIONS

REFLECTIONS

👏 I am grateful for …

⛰️ I will accomplish …

⚙️ I need to work on …

DATE	TIME
LOCATION	DURATION
METHOD	MANTRA

MEDITATION POSITION

☐ ☐ ☐ ☐ ☐

MEDITATION FOCUS

MOOD WHEEL

Inner ring: HAPPY, SAD, DISGUST, ANGER, FEAR, SURPRISE

Outer ring: OPTIMISTIC, PROUD, GUILTY, DEPRESSED, LONELY, DISAPPROVAL, AWFUL, DISAPPOINTED, AGGRESSIVE, MAD, HURT, SCARED, HUMILIATED, INSECURE, AMAZED, EXCITED, CONFUSED, PEACEFUL

THOUGHTS & INSIGHTS

QUALITY AND INTENSITY

FOCUS AND BREATHING — 1 — 2 — 3 — 4 — 5 — 6 — 7 — 8 — 9 — 10

VISIONS AND EMOTIONS

REFLECTIONS

I am grateful for ...

I will accomplish ...

I need to work on ...

DATE	TIME
LOCATION	DURATION
METHOD	MANTRA

MEDITATION POSITION

☐　　☐　　☐　　☐　　☐

MEDITATION FOCUS

MOOD WHEEL

Mood wheel with core emotions: HAPPY, SAD, DISGUST, ANGER, FEAR, SURPRISE
Outer emotions: OPTIMISTIC, PROUD, GUILTY, DEPRESSED, LONELY, DISAPPROVAL, AWFUL, DISAPPOINTED, AGGRESSIVE, MAD, HURT, SCARED, HUMILIATED, INSECURE, AMAZED, EXCITED, CONFUSED, PEACEFUL

THOUGHTS & INSIGHTS

QUALITY AND INTENSITY

FOCUS AND BREATHING　　1 — 2 — 3 — 4 — 5 — 6 — 7 — 8 — 9 — 10

VISIONS AND EMOTIONS

REFLECTIONS

I am grateful for …

I will accomplish …

I need to work on …

	DATE		TIME
	LOCATION		DURATION
	METHOD		MANTRA

MEDITATION POSITION

☐ ☐ ☐ ☐ ☐

MEDITATION FOCUS

MOOD WHEEL

Mood wheel with inner emotions: HAPPY, SAD, DISGUST, ANGER, FEAR, SURPRISE. Outer emotions: OPTIMISTIC, PROUD, GUILTY, DEPRESSED, LONELY, DISAPPROVAL, AWFUL, DISAPPOINTED, AGGRESSIVE, MAD, HURT, SCARED, HUMILIATED, INSECURE, AMAZED, EXCITED, CONFUSED, PEACEFUL.

THOUGHTS & INSIGHTS

QUALITY AND INTENSITY

FOCUS AND BREATHING — 1 — 2 — 3 — 4 — 5 — 6 — 7 — 8 — 9 — 10

VISIONS AND EMOTIONS

REFLECTIONS

I am grateful for …

I will accomplish …

I need to work on …

📅 DATE	🕐 TIME
📍 LOCATION	⏱️ DURATION
🧘 METHOD	✺ MANTRA

MEDITATION POSITION

🧘 ☐	🪑 ☐	🚶 ☐	🛌 ☐	🤸 ☐

MEDITATION FOCUS

MOOD WHEEL

(Mood wheel with inner sections: HAPPY, SAD, DISGUST, ANGER, FEAR, SURPRISE; outer labels: OPTIMISTIC, PROUD, GUILTY, DEPRESSED, LONELY, DISAPPROVAL, AWFUL, DISAPPOINTED, AGGRESSIVE, MAD, HURT, SCARED, HUMILIATED, INSECURE, AMAZED, EXCITED, CONFUSED, PEACEFUL)

THOUGHTS & INSIGHTS

QUALITY AND INTENSITY

	1	2	3	4	5	6	7	8	9	10
FOCUS AND BREATHING	○	○	○	○	○	○	○	○	○	○
VISIONS AND EMOTIONS	○	○	○	○	○	○	○	○	○	○

REFLECTIONS

👐 I am grateful for ...

⛰️ I will accomplish ...

⚙️ I need to work on ...

	DATE		TIME
	LOCATION		DURATION
	METHOD		MANTRA

MEDITATION POSITION

☐ ☐ ☐ ☐ ☐

MEDITATION FOCUS

MOOD WHEEL

Mood wheel sections: HAPPY (OPTIMISTIC, PEACEFUL, PROUD), SAD (GUILTY, DEPRESSED, LONELY), SURPRISE (CONFUSED, EXCITED, AMAZED), DISGUST (DISAPPROVAL, AWFUL, DISAPPOINTED), FEAR (INSECURE, HUMILIATED, SCARED), ANGER (HURT, MAD, AGGRESSIVE)

THOUGHTS & INSIGHTS

QUALITY AND INTENSITY

	FOCUS AND BREATHING	1 — 2 — 3 — 4 — 5 — 6 — 7 — 8 — 9 — 10
	VISIONS AND EMOTIONS	

REFLECTIONS

	I am grateful for ...
	I will accomplish ...
	I need to work on ...

	DATE		TIME
	LOCATION		DURATION
	METHOD		MANTRA

MEDITATION POSITION

☐ ☐ ☐ ☐ ☐

MEDITATION FOCUS

MOOD WHEEL

PROUD, OPTIMISTIC, PEACEFUL, CONFUSED, EXCITED, AMAZED, INSECURE, HUMILIATED, SCARED, HURT, MAD, AGGRESSIVE, DISAPPOINTED, AWFUL, DISAPPROVAL, LONELY, DEPRESSED, GUILTY

HAPPY, SAD, DISGUST, ANGER, FEAR, SURPRISE

THOUGHTS & INSIGHTS

QUALITY AND INTENSITY

FOCUS AND BREATHING   1 — 2 — 3 — 4 — 5 — 6 — 7 — 8 — 9 — 10
VISIONS AND EMOTIONS

REFLECTIONS

I am grateful for ...

I will accomplish ...

I need to work on ...

DATE	TIME
LOCATION	DURATION
METHOD	MANTRA

MEDITATION POSITION

☐ ☐ ☐ ☐ ☐

MEDITATION FOCUS

MOOD WHEEL

THOUGHTS & INSIGHTS

QUALITY AND INTENSITY

FOCUS AND BREATHING — 1 — 2 — 3 — 4 — 5 — 6 — 7 — 8 — 9 — 10

VISIONS AND EMOTIONS

REFLECTIONS

I am grateful for …

I will accomplish …

I need to work on …

📅 DATE	🕐 TIME
📍 LOCATION	⏱️ DURATION
🧘 METHOD	❁ MANTRA

MEDITATION POSITION

🧘 ☐	🪑 ☐	🚶 ☐	🛌 ☐	🤸 ☐

MEDITATION FOCUS

MOOD WHEEL

Mood wheel with inner emotions: HAPPY, SAD, SURPRISE, DISGUST, FEAR, ANGER
Outer emotions: OPTIMISTIC, PROUD, GUILTY, DEPRESSED, LONELY, DISAPPROVAL, AWFUL, DISAPPOINTED, AGGRESSIVE, MAD, HURT, SCARED, HUMILIATED, INSECURE, AMAZED, EXCITED, CONFUSED, PEACEFUL

THOUGHTS & INSIGHTS

QUALITY AND INTENSITY

FOCUS AND BREATHING — 1 — 2 — 3 — 4 — 5 — 6 — 7 — 8 — 9 — 10

VISIONS AND EMOTIONS

REFLECTIONS

🙏 I am grateful for …

🏔️ I will accomplish …

⚙️ I need to work on …

📅 DATE	🕐 TIME
📍 LOCATION	⏱️ DURATION
🧘 METHOD	✺ MANTRA

MEDITATION POSITION

🧘 ☐	🪑 ☐	🧍 ☐	🛌 ☐	🤸 ☐

MEDITATION FOCUS

MOOD WHEEL

THOUGHTS & INSIGHTS

QUALITY AND INTENSITY

FOCUS AND BREATHING — 1 — 2 — 3 — 4 — 5 — 6 — 7 — 8 — 9 — 10

VISIONS AND EMOTIONS

REFLECTIONS

I am grateful for …

I will accomplish …

I need to work on …

DATE	TIME
LOCATION	DURATION
METHOD	MANTRA

MEDITATION POSITION

☐ ☐ ☐ ☐ ☐

MEDITATION FOCUS

MOOD WHEEL

- OPTIMISTIC
- PROUD
- GUILTY
- PEACEFUL
- DEPRESSED
- LONELY
- CONFUSED
- HAPPY
- SAD
- DISAPPROVAL
- EXCITED
- SURPRISE
- DISGUST
- AWFUL
- AMAZED
- FEAR
- ANGER
- DISAPPOINTED
- INSECURE
- AGGRESSIVE
- HUMILIATED
- SCARED
- HURT
- MAD

THOUGHTS & INSIGHTS

QUALITY AND INTENSITY

FOCUS AND BREATHING

1 — 2 — 3 — 4 — 5 — 6 — 7 — 8 — 9 — 10

VISIONS AND EMOTIONS

REFLECTIONS

I am grateful for …

I will accomplish …

I need to work on …

📅 DATE	🕐 TIME
📍 LOCATION	⏱️ DURATION
🧘 METHOD	🪷 MANTRA

MEDITATION POSITION

☐ ☐ ☐ ☐ ☐

MEDITATION FOCUS

MOOD WHEEL

Mood wheel with inner emotions: HAPPY, SAD, DISGUST, ANGER, FEAR, SURPRISE
Outer emotions: OPTIMISTIC, PROUD, GUILTY, DEPRESSED, LONELY, DISAPPROVAL, AWFUL, DISAPPOINTED, AGGRESSIVE, MAD, HURT, SCARED, HUMILIATED, INSECURE, AMAZED, EXCITED, CONFUSED, PEACEFUL

THOUGHTS & INSIGHTS

QUALITY AND INTENSITY

FOCUS AND BREATHING   1 — 2 — 3 — 4 — 5 — 6 — 7 — 8 — 9 — 10

VISIONS AND EMOTIONS

REFLECTIONS

🙏 I am grateful for ...

⛰️ I will accomplish ...

⚙️ I need to work on ...

📅 DATE	🕐 TIME
📍 LOCATION	⏱️ DURATION
🧘 METHOD	✳️ MANTRA

MEDITATION POSITION

🧘 ☐	🪑 ☐	🧍 ☐	🛌 ☐	🤸 ☐

MEDITATION FOCUS

MOOD WHEEL

(Wheel with inner emotions: HAPPY, SAD, SURPRISE, DISGUST, FEAR, ANGER; outer emotions: OPTIMISTIC, PROUD, GUILTY, DEPRESSED, LONELY, DISAPPROVAL, AWFUL, DISAPPOINTED, AGGRESSIVE, MAD, HURT, SCARED, HUMILIATED, INSECURE, AMAZED, EXCITED, CONFUSED, PEACEFUL)

THOUGHTS & INSIGHTS

QUALITY AND INTENSITY

FOCUS AND BREATHING	1 — 2 — 3 — 4 — 5 — 6 — 7 — 8 — 9 — 10
VISIONS AND EMOTIONS	1 — 2 — 3 — 4 — 5 — 6 — 7 — 8 — 9 — 10

REFLECTIONS

👏 I am grateful for …

⛰️ I will accomplish …

📈 I need to work on …

📅 DATE	🕐 TIME
📍 LOCATION	⏱️ DURATION
🧘 METHOD	⚙️ MANTRA

MEDITATION POSITION

☐ ☐ ☐ ☐ ☐

MEDITATION FOCUS

MOOD WHEEL

Inner ring: HAPPY, SAD, DISGUST, ANGER, FEAR, SURPRISE

Middle ring: OPTIMISTIC, PROUD, GUILTY, DEPRESSED, LONELY, DISAPPROVAL, AWFUL, DISAPPOINTED, AGGRESSIVE, MAD, HURT, SCARED, HUMILIATED, INSECURE, AMAZED, EXCITED, CONFUSED, PEACEFUL

THOUGHTS & INSIGHTS

QUALITY AND INTENSITY

FOCUS AND BREATHING — 1 — 2 — 3 — 4 — 5 — 6 — 7 — 8 — 9 — 10

VISIONS AND EMOTIONS

REFLECTIONS

I am grateful for …

I will accomplish …

I need to work on …

DATE	TIME
LOCATION	DURATION
METHOD	MANTRA

MEDITATION POSITION

☐   ☐   ☐   ☐   ☐

MEDITATION FOCUS

MOOD WHEEL

Mood wheel with core emotions: HAPPY, SAD, DISGUST, ANGER, FEAR, SURPRISE. Secondary emotions: OPTIMISTIC, PROUD, GUILTY, DEPRESSED, LONELY, DISAPPROVAL, AWFUL, DISAPPOINTED, AGGRESSIVE, MAD, HURT, SCARED, HUMILIATED, INSECURE, AMAZED, EXCITED, CONFUSED, PEACEFUL.

THOUGHTS & INSIGHTS

QUALITY AND INTENSITY

FOCUS AND BREATHING — 1 — 2 — 3 — 4 — 5 — 6 — 7 — 8 — 9 — 10

VISIONS AND EMOTIONS

REFLECTIONS

I am grateful for …

I will accomplish …

I need to work on …

📅 DATE	🕐 TIME
📍 LOCATION	⏱️ DURATION
🧘 METHOD	✺ MANTRA

MEDITATION POSITION

🧘 ☐   🪑 ☐   🧍 ☐   🛌 ☐   🤸 ☐

MEDITATION FOCUS

THOUGHTS & INSIGHTS

MOOD WHEEL

- PROUD
- GUILTY
- OPTIMISTIC
- DEPRESSED
- PEACEFUL
- LONELY
- CONFUSED
- DISAPPROVAL
- HAPPY / SAD
- EXCITED
- SURPRISE / DISGUST
- AWFUL
- AMAZED
- FEAR / ANGER
- DISAPPOINTED
- INSECURE
- AGGRESSIVE
- HUMILIATED
- MAD
- SCARED
- HURT

QUALITY AND INTENSITY

FOCUS AND BREATHING   ○─○─○─○─○─○─○─○─○─○
                                 1─2─3─4─5─6─7─8─9─10

VISIONS AND EMOTIONS   ○─○─○─○─○─○─○─○─○─○

REFLECTIONS

🙏 I am grateful for …

⛰️ I will accomplish …

⚙️ I need to work on …

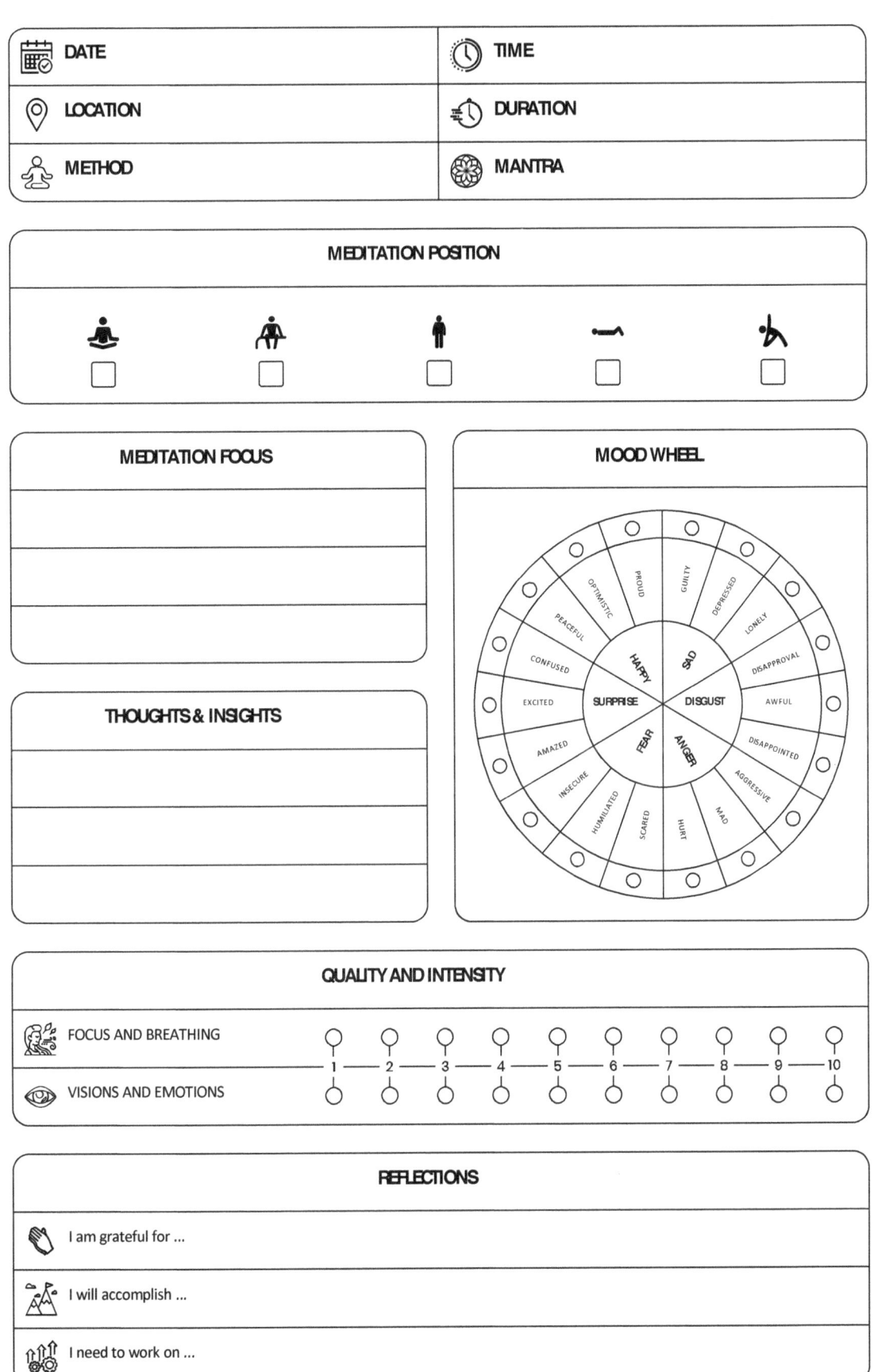

📅 DATE	🕐 TIME
📍 LOCATION	⏱️ DURATION
🧘 METHOD	🌸 MANTRA

MEDITATION POSITION

☐ ☐ ☐ ☐ ☐

MEDITATION FOCUS

MOOD WHEEL

Inner ring: HAPPY, SAD, DISGUST, ANGER, FEAR, SURPRISE

Outer ring: OPTIMISTIC, PROUD, GUILTY, DEPRESSED, LONELY, DISAPPROVAL, AWFUL, DISAPPOINTED, AGGRESSIVE, MAD, HURT, SCARED, HUMILIATED, INSECURE, AMAZED, EXCITED, CONFUSED, PEACEFUL

THOUGHTS & INSIGHTS

QUALITY AND INTENSITY

FOCUS AND BREATHING — 1 2 3 4 5 6 7 8 9 10

VISIONS AND EMOTIONS — 1 2 3 4 5 6 7 8 9 10

REFLECTIONS

I am grateful for …

I will accomplish …

I need to work on …

📅 DATE	🕐 TIME
📍 LOCATION	⏱️ DURATION
🧘 METHOD	❄️ MANTRA

MEDITATION POSITION

☐ ☐ ☐ ☐ ☐

MEDITATION FOCUS

MOOD WHEEL

Mood wheel with core emotions: HAPPY, SAD, SURPRISE, DISGUST, FEAR, ANGER, and surrounding feelings: OPTIMISTIC, PROUD, GUILTY, DEPRESSED, PEACEFUL, LONELY, CONFUSED, DISAPPROVAL, EXCITED, AWFUL, AMAZED, DISAPPOINTED, INSECURE, AGGRESSIVE, HUMILIATED, MAD, SCARED, HURT.

THOUGHTS & INSIGHTS

QUALITY AND INTENSITY

	1	2	3	4	5	6	7	8	9	10
FOCUS AND BREATHING	○	○	○	○	○	○	○	○	○	○
VISIONS AND EMOTIONS	○	○	○	○	○	○	○	○	○	○

REFLECTIONS

🙏 I am grateful for …

🏔️ I will accomplish …

⚙️ I need to work on …

📅 DATE	🕐 TIME
📍 LOCATION	⏱️ DURATION
🧘 METHOD	❀ MANTRA

MEDITATION POSITION

🧘	🪑	🧍	🛌	🤸
☐	☐	☐	☐	☐

MEDITATION FOCUS

MOOD WHEEL

Mood wheel with emotions: OPTIMISTIC, PROUD, GUILTY, DEPRESSED, PEACEFUL, LONELY, CONFUSED, DISAPPROVAL, HAPPY, SAD, EXCITED, SURPRISE, DISGUST, AWFUL, AMAZED, FEAR, ANGER, DISAPPOINTED, INSECURE, AGGRESSIVE, HUMILIATED, SCARED, HURT, MAD

THOUGHTS & INSIGHTS

QUALITY AND INTENSITY

FOCUS AND BREATHING — 1 — 2 — 3 — 4 — 5 — 6 — 7 — 8 — 9 — 10

VISIONS AND EMOTIONS

REFLECTIONS

🙏 I am grateful for …

⛰️ I will accomplish …

📈 I need to work on …

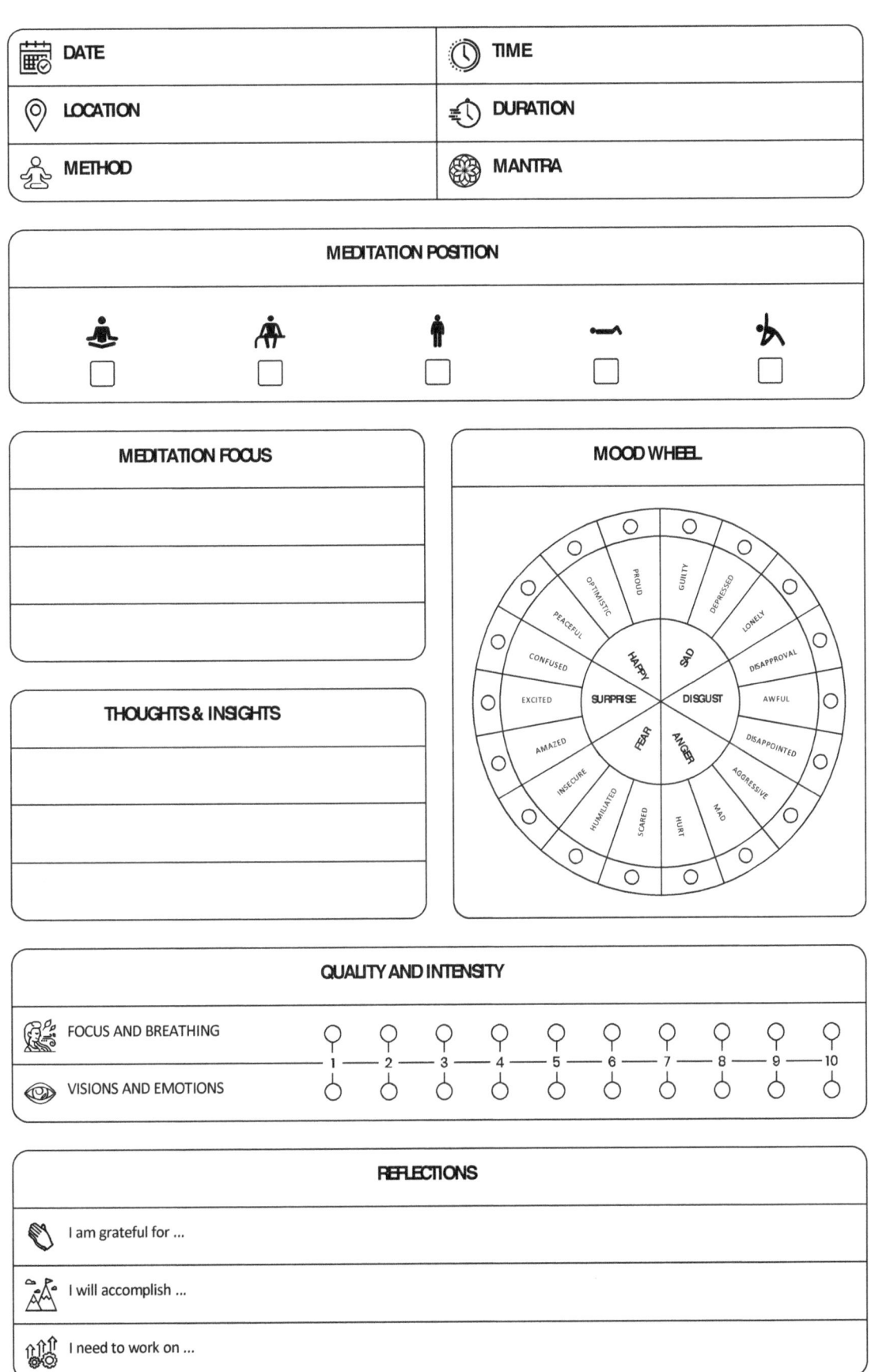

📅 DATE	🕐 TIME
📍 LOCATION	⏱ DURATION
🧘 METHOD	✸ MANTRA

MEDITATION POSITION

☐ ☐ ☐ ☐ ☐

MEDITATION FOCUS

MOOD WHEEL

Mood wheel with inner emotions: HAPPY, SAD, DISGUST, ANGER, FEAR, SURPRISE

Outer emotions: OPTIMISTIC, PROUD, GUILTY, DEPRESSED, LONELY, DISAPPROVAL, AWFUL, DISAPPOINTED, MAD, HURT, SCARED, HUMILIATED, INSECURE, AMAZED, EXCITED, CONFUSED, PEACEFUL

THOUGHTS & INSIGHTS

QUALITY AND INTENSITY

	1	2	3	4	5	6	7	8	9	10
FOCUS AND BREATHING	○	○	○	○	○	○	○	○	○	○
VISIONS AND EMOTIONS	○	○	○	○	○	○	○	○	○	○

REFLECTIONS

🙏 I am grateful for ...

⛰ I will accomplish ...

⚙ I need to work on ...

DATE	TIME
LOCATION	DURATION
METHOD	MANTRA

MEDITATION POSITION

☐   ☐   ☐   ☐   ☐

MEDITATION FOCUS

MOOD WHEEL

Mood wheel with core emotions: HAPPY, SAD, DISGUST, ANGER, FEAR, SURPRISE
Outer emotions: OPTIMISTIC, PROUD, GUILTY, DEPRESSED, LONELY, DISAPPROVAL, AWFUL, DISAPPOINTED, AGGRESSIVE, MAD, HURT, SCARED, HUMILIATED, INSECURE, AMAZED, EXCITED, CONFUSED, PEACEFUL

THOUGHTS & INSIGHTS

QUALITY AND INTENSITY

FOCUS AND BREATHING — 1 — 2 — 3 — 4 — 5 — 6 — 7 — 8 — 9 — 10

VISIONS AND EMOTIONS

REFLECTIONS

I am grateful for …

I will accomplish …

I need to work on …

📅 DATE	🕐 TIME
📍 LOCATION	⏱ DURATION
🧘 METHOD	❁ MANTRA

MEDITATION POSITION

☐ ☐ ☐ ☐ ☐

MEDITATION FOCUS

MOOD WHEEL

Mood wheel with inner emotions: HAPPY, SAD, SURPRISE, DISGUST, FEAR, ANGER
Middle ring: OPTIMISTIC, PROUD, GUILTY, DEPRESSED, LONELY, DISAPPROVAL, AWFUL, DISAPPOINTED, AGGRESSIVE, MAD, HURT, SCARED, HUMILIATED, INSECURE, AMAZED, EXCITED, CONFUSED, PEACEFUL

THOUGHTS & INSIGHTS

QUALITY AND INTENSITY

FOCUS AND BREATHING — 1 — 2 — 3 — 4 — 5 — 6 — 7 — 8 — 9 — 10

VISIONS AND EMOTIONS — 1 — 2 — 3 — 4 — 5 — 6 — 7 — 8 — 9 — 10

REFLECTIONS

🙏 I am grateful for …

⛰ I will accomplish …

📈 I need to work on …

DATE	TIME
LOCATION	DURATION
METHOD	MANTRA

MEDITATION POSITION

☐ ☐ ☐ ☐ ☐

MEDITATION FOCUS

MOOD WHEEL

Mood wheel with emotions: HAPPY (optimistic, proud, peaceful), SAD (guilty, depressed, lonely), DISGUST (disapproval, awful, disappointed), ANGER (aggressive, mad, hurt), FEAR (scared, humiliated, insecure), SURPRISE (amazed, excited, confused)

THOUGHTS & INSIGHTS

QUALITY AND INTENSITY

FOCUS AND BREATHING — 1 — 2 — 3 — 4 — 5 — 6 — 7 — 8 — 9 — 10

VISIONS AND EMOTIONS

REFLECTIONS

I am grateful for …

I will accomplish …

I need to work on …

📅 DATE	🕐 TIME
📍 LOCATION	⏱️ DURATION
🧘 METHOD	🕉️ MANTRA

MEDITATION POSITION

☐ ☐ ☐ ☐ ☐

MEDITATION FOCUS

MOOD WHEEL

(Mood wheel with emotions: HAPPY, SAD, DISGUST, ANGER, FEAR, SURPRISE in center; outer emotions include OPTIMISTIC, PROUD, GUILTY, DEPRESSED, LONELY, DISAPPROVAL, AWFUL, DISAPPOINTED, AGGRESSIVE, MAD, HURT, SCARED, HUMILIATED, INSECURE, AMAZED, EXCITED, CONFUSED, PEACEFUL)

THOUGHTS & INSIGHTS

QUALITY AND INTENSITY

	1	2	3	4	5	6	7	8	9	10
FOCUS AND BREATHING	○	○	○	○	○	○	○	○	○	○
VISIONS AND EMOTIONS	○	○	○	○	○	○	○	○	○	○

REFLECTIONS

🙏 I am grateful for …

⛰️ I will accomplish …

⚙️ I need to work on …

📅 DATE	🕐 TIME
📍 LOCATION	⏱ DURATION
🧘 METHOD	❄ MANTRA

MEDITATION POSITION

| 🧘 ☐ | 🧎 ☐ | 🧍 ☐ | 🛌 ☐ | 🤸 ☐ |

MEDITATION FOCUS

MOOD WHEEL

Mood wheel with inner emotions: HAPPY, SAD, SURPRISE, DISGUST, FEAR, ANGER
Outer emotions: OPTIMISTIC, PROUD, GUILTY, DEPRESSED, LONELY, DISAPPROVAL, AWFUL, DISAPPOINTED, AGGRESSIVE, MAD, HURT, SCARED, HUMILIATED, INSECURE, AMAZED, EXCITED, CONFUSED, PEACEFUL

THOUGHTS & INSIGHTS

QUALITY AND INTENSITY

	1	2	3	4	5	6	7	8	9	10
FOCUS AND BREATHING	○	○	○	○	○	○	○	○	○	○
VISIONS AND EMOTIONS	○	○	○	○	○	○	○	○	○	○

REFLECTIONS

👐 I am grateful for ...

⛰ I will accomplish ...

📈 I need to work on ...

DATE	TIME
LOCATION	DURATION
METHOD	MANTRA

MEDITATION POSITION

☐ ☐ ☐ ☐ ☐

MEDITATION FOCUS

MOOD WHEEL

Mood Wheel: HAPPY, SAD, DISGUST, ANGER, FEAR, SURPRISE — OPTIMISTIC, PROUD, GUILTY, DEPRESSED, LONELY, DISAPPROVAL, AWFUL, DISAPPOINTED, AGGRESSIVE, MAD, HURT, SCARED, HUMILIATED, INSECURE, AMAZED, EXCITED, CONFUSED, PEACEFUL

THOUGHTS & INSIGHTS

QUALITY AND INTENSITY

FOCUS AND BREATHING — 1 — 2 — 3 — 4 — 5 — 6 — 7 — 8 — 9 — 10

VISIONS AND EMOTIONS

REFLECTIONS

I am grateful for …

I will accomplish …

I need to work on …

📅 DATE	🕐 TIME
📍 LOCATION	⏱️ DURATION
🧘 METHOD	✺ MANTRA

MEDITATION POSITION

☐ ☐ ☐ ☐ ☐

MEDITATION FOCUS

MOOD WHEEL

THOUGHTS & INSIGHTS

QUALITY AND INTENSITY

FOCUS AND BREATHING — 1 — 2 — 3 — 4 — 5 — 6 — 7 — 8 — 9 — 10

VISIONS AND EMOTIONS

REFLECTIONS

I am grateful for …

I will accomplish …

I need to work on …

📅	DATE	🕐	TIME
📍	LOCATION	⏱️	DURATION
🧘	METHOD	❋	MANTRA

MEDITATION POSITION

☐ ☐ ☐ ☐ ☐

MEDITATION FOCUS

MOOD WHEEL

THOUGHTS & INSIGHTS

QUALITY AND INTENSITY

FOCUS AND BREATHING 1 — 2 — 3 — 4 — 5 — 6 — 7 — 8 — 9 — 10

VISIONS AND EMOTIONS

REFLECTIONS

- I am grateful for …
- I will accomplish …
- I need to work on …

📅 DATE	🕐 TIME
📍 LOCATION	⏱️ DURATION
🧘 METHOD	🌸 MANTRA

MEDITATION POSITION

☐ ☐ ☐ ☐ ☐

MEDITATION FOCUS

MOOD WHEEL

- PROUD
- OPTIMISTIC
- PEACEFUL
- CONFUSED
- EXCITED
- AMAZED
- INSECURE
- HUMILIATED
- SCARED
- HURT
- MAD
- AGGRESSIVE
- DISAPPOINTED
- AWFUL
- DISAPPROVAL
- LONELY
- DEPRESSED
- GUILTY

Center: HAPPY, SAD, SURPRISE, DISGUST, FEAR, ANGER

THOUGHTS & INSIGHTS

QUALITY AND INTENSITY

	1 — 2 — 3 — 4 — 5 — 6 — 7 — 8 — 9 — 10
FOCUS AND BREATHING	○ ○ ○ ○ ○ ○ ○ ○ ○ ○
VISIONS AND EMOTIONS	○ ○ ○ ○ ○ ○ ○ ○ ○ ○

REFLECTIONS

👏 I am grateful for …

⛰️ I will accomplish …

📈 I need to work on …

📅 DATE		🕐 TIME	
📍 LOCATION		⏱ DURATION	
🧘 METHOD		❀ MANTRA	

MEDITATION POSITION

🧘	🪑	🧍	🛌	🤸
☐	☐	☐	☐	☐

MEDITATION FOCUS

MOOD WHEEL

Mood wheel with emotions: OPTIMISTIC, PROUD, GUILTY, DEPRESSED, PEACEFUL, LONELY, CONFUSED, DISAPPROVAL, EXCITED, AWFUL, AMAZED, DISAPPOINTED, INSECURE, AGGRESSIVE, HUMILIATED, SCARED, HURT, MAD. Central emotions: HAPPY, SAD, SURPRISE, DISGUST, FEAR, ANGER.

THOUGHTS & INSIGHTS

QUALITY AND INTENSITY

FOCUS AND BREATHING — 1 — 2 — 3 — 4 — 5 — 6 — 7 — 8 — 9 — 10

VISIONS AND EMOTIONS — 1 — 2 — 3 — 4 — 5 — 6 — 7 — 8 — 9 — 10

REFLECTIONS

🙏 I am grateful for ...

⛰ I will accomplish ...

📈 I need to work on ...

	DATE		TIME
	LOCATION		DURATION
	METHOD		MANTRA

MEDITATION POSITION

☐   ☐   ☐   ☐   ☐

MEDITATION FOCUS

MOOD WHEEL

Mood wheel with inner emotions: HAPPY, SAD, DISGUST, ANGER, FEAR, SURPRISE. Outer emotions: OPTIMISTIC, PROUD, GUILTY, DEPRESSED, LONELY, DISAPPROVAL, AWFUL, DISAPPOINTED, AGGRESSIVE, MAD, HURT, SCARED, HUMILIATED, INSECURE, AMAZED, EXCITED, CONFUSED, PEACEFUL.

THOUGHTS & INSIGHTS

QUALITY AND INTENSITY

FOCUS AND BREATHING

1 — 2 — 3 — 4 — 5 — 6 — 7 — 8 — 9 — 10

VISIONS AND EMOTIONS

REFLECTIONS

I am grateful for …

I will accomplish …

I need to work on …

📅	DATE	🕐	TIME
📍	LOCATION	⏱	DURATION
🧘	METHOD	❋	MANTRA

MEDITATION POSITION

☐ ☐ ☐ ☐ ☐

MEDITATION FOCUS

MOOD WHEEL

Mood wheel with core emotions: HAPPY, SAD, DISGUST, ANGER, FEAR, SURPRISE. Outer labels: OPTIMISTIC, PROUD, GUILTY, DEPRESSED, LONELY, DISAPPROVAL, AWFUL, DISAPPOINTED, AGGRESSIVE, MAD, HURT, SCARED, HUMILIATED, INSECURE, AMAZED, EXCITED, CONFUSED, PEACEFUL.

THOUGHTS & INSIGHTS

QUALITY AND INTENSITY

FOCUS AND BREATHING   ○—○—○—○—○—○—○—○—○—○
                                        1 2 3 4 5 6 7 8 9 10
VISIONS AND EMOTIONS ○ ○ ○ ○ ○ ○ ○ ○ ○ ○

REFLECTIONS

🙏 I am grateful for ...

⛰ I will accomplish ...

⚙ I need to work on ...

📅 DATE	🕐 TIME
📍 LOCATION	⏱️ DURATION
🧘 METHOD	✳️ MANTRA

MEDITATION POSITION

☐   ☐   ☐   ☐   ☐

MEDITATION FOCUS

MOOD WHEEL

HAPPY · SAD · SURPRISE · DISGUST · FEAR · ANGER

OPTIMISTIC, PROUD, GUILTY, DEPRESSED, PEACEFUL, LONELY, CONFUSED, DISAPPROVAL, EXCITED, AWFUL, AMAZED, DISAPPOINTED, INSECURE, AGGRESSIVE, HUMILIATED, SCARED, HURT, MAD

THOUGHTS & INSIGHTS

QUALITY AND INTENSITY

FOCUS AND BREATHING — 1 — 2 — 3 — 4 — 5 — 6 — 7 — 8 — 9 — 10

VISIONS AND EMOTIONS

REFLECTIONS

- I am grateful for ...
- I will accomplish ...
- I need to work on ...

📅 DATE		🕐 TIME	
📍 LOCATION		⏱ DURATION	
🧘 METHOD		❁ MANTRA	

MEDITATION POSITION

🧘	🪑	🧍	🛌	🤸
☐	☐	☐	☐	☐

MEDITATION FOCUS

MOOD WHEEL

Mood wheel with inner emotions: HAPPY, SAD, DISGUST, ANGER, FEAR, SURPRISE
Outer ring: OPTIMISTIC, PROUD, GUILTY, DEPRESSED, LONELY, DISAPPROVAL, AWFUL, DISAPPOINTED, AGGRESSIVE, MAD, HURT, SCARED, HUMILIATED, INSECURE, AMAZED, EXCITED, CONFUSED, PEACEFUL

THOUGHTS & INSIGHTS

QUALITY AND INTENSITY

FOCUS AND BREATHING   1 — 2 — 3 — 4 — 5 — 6 — 7 — 8 — 9 — 10
VISIONS AND EMOTIONS

REFLECTIONS

🙏 I am grateful for …

⛰ I will accomplish …

⚙ I need to work on …

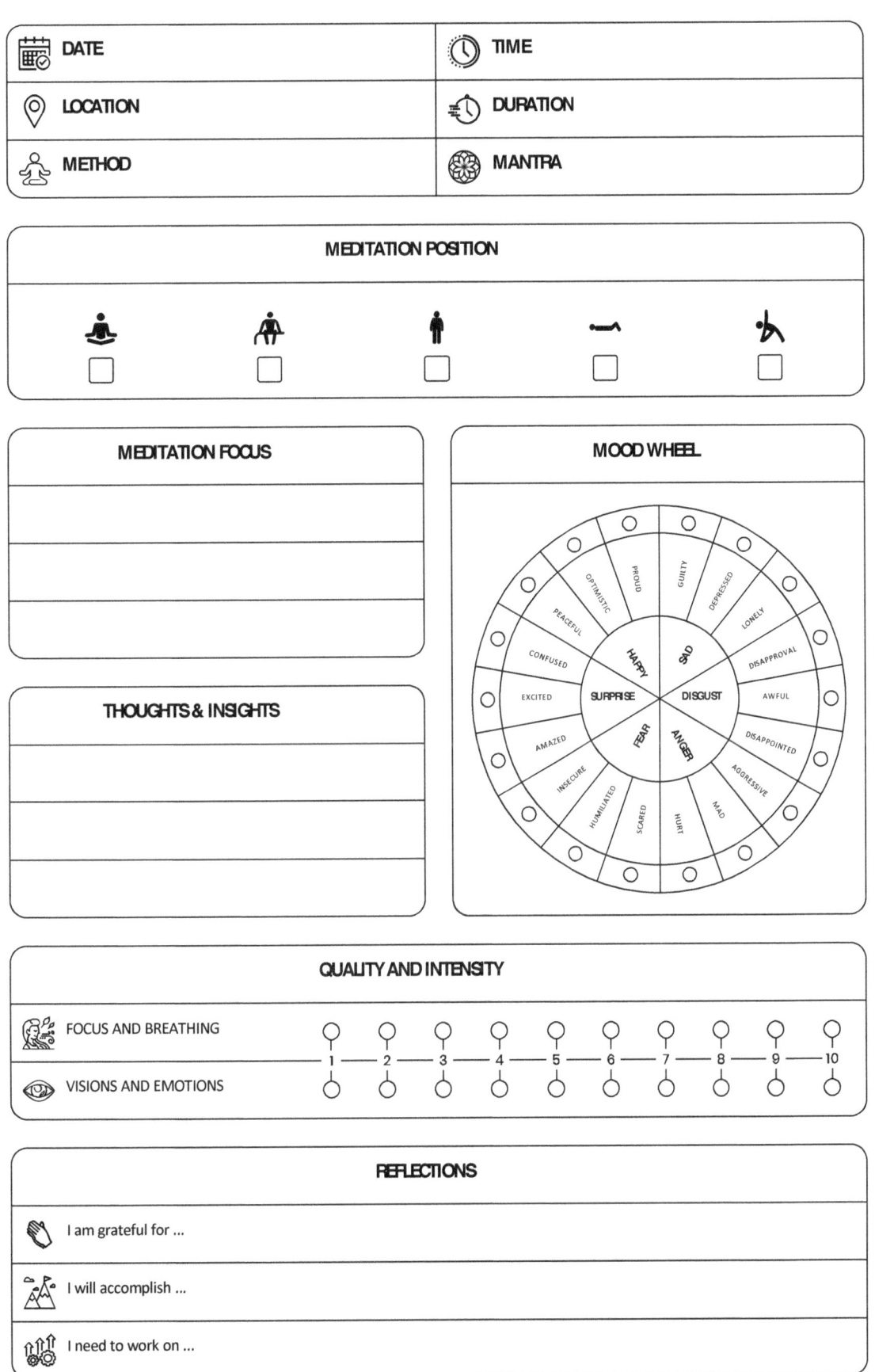

📅 DATE	🕐 TIME
📍 LOCATION	⏱️ DURATION
🧘 METHOD	❁ MANTRA

MEDITATION POSITION

| 🧘 ☐ | 🪑 ☐ | 🧍 ☐ | 🛌 ☐ | 🤸 ☐ |

MEDITATION FOCUS

MOOD WHEEL

THOUGHTS & INSIGHTS

QUALITY AND INTENSITY

FOCUS AND BREATHING — 1 — 2 — 3 — 4 — 5 — 6 — 7 — 8 — 9 — 10

VISIONS AND EMOTIONS — 1 — 2 — 3 — 4 — 5 — 6 — 7 — 8 — 9 — 10

REFLECTIONS

🙌 I am grateful for …

⛰️ I will accomplish …

⚙️ I need to work on …

📅	**DATE**	🕐	**TIME**
📍	**LOCATION**	⏱️	**DURATION**
🧘	**METHOD**	❄️	**MANTRA**

MEDITATION POSITION

🧘 ☐   🪑 ☐   🧍 ☐   🛌 ☐   🤸 ☐

MEDITATION FOCUS

MOOD WHEEL

(Mood wheel with inner emotions: HAPPY, SAD, DISGUST, ANGER, FEAR, SURPRISE; outer emotions: OPTIMISTIC, PROUD, GUILTY, DEPRESSED, LONELY, DISAPPROVAL, AWFUL, DISAPPOINTED, AGGRESSIVE, MAD, HURT, SCARED, HUMILIATED, INSECURE, AMAZED, EXCITED, CONFUSED, PEACEFUL)

THOUGHTS & INSIGHTS

QUALITY AND INTENSITY

FOCUS AND BREATHING   1 — 2 — 3 — 4 — 5 — 6 — 7 — 8 — 9 — 10

VISIONS AND EMOTIONS

REFLECTIONS

🙏 I am grateful for …

⛰️ I will accomplish …

⚙️ I need to work on …

📅	DATE	🕐 TIME	
📍	LOCATION	⏱️ DURATION	
🧘	METHOD	✳️ MANTRA	

MEDITATION POSITION

☐ ☐ ☐ ☐ ☐

MEDITATION FOCUS

MOOD WHEEL

Mood wheel with inner emotions: HAPPY, SAD, DISGUST, ANGER, FEAR, SURPRISE
Outer emotions: OPTIMISTIC, PROUD, GUILTY, DEPRESSED, LONELY, DISAPPROVAL, AWFUL, DISAPPOINTED, AGGRESSIVE, MAD, HURT, SCARED, HUMILIATED, INSECURE, AMAZED, EXCITED, CONFUSED, PEACEFUL

THOUGHTS & INSIGHTS

QUALITY AND INTENSITY

FOCUS AND BREATHING   1 — 2 — 3 — 4 — 5 — 6 — 7 — 8 — 9 — 10
VISIONS AND EMOTIONS

REFLECTIONS

🙏 I am grateful for …

⛰️ I will accomplish …

⚙️ I need to work on …

	DATE		TIME
	LOCATION		DURATION
	METHOD		MANTRA

MEDITATION POSITION

☐ ☐ ☐ ☐ ☐

MEDITATION FOCUS

MOOD WHEEL

Mood wheel with core emotions: HAPPY, SAD, DISGUST, ANGER, FEAR, SURPRISE. Outer labels: OPTIMISTIC, PROUD, GUILTY, DEPRESSED, LONELY, DISAPPROVAL, AWFUL, DISAPPOINTED, AGGRESSIVE, MAD, HURT, SCARED, HUMILIATED, INSECURE, AMAZED, EXCITED, CONFUSED, PEACEFUL.

THOUGHTS & INSIGHTS

QUALITY AND INTENSITY

FOCUS AND BREATHING ○ ○ ○ ○ ○ ○ ○ ○ ○ ○
1 — 2 — 3 — 4 — 5 — 6 — 7 — 8 — 9 — 10
VISIONS AND EMOTIONS ○ ○ ○ ○ ○ ○ ○ ○ ○ ○

REFLECTIONS

I am grateful for …

I will accomplish …

I need to work on …

📅 DATE	🕐 TIME
📍 LOCATION	⏱️ DURATION
🧘 METHOD	✸ MANTRA

MEDITATION POSITION

🧘 ☐	🪑 ☐	🧍 ☐	🛌 ☐	🤸 ☐

MEDITATION FOCUS

THOUGHTS & INSIGHTS

MOOD WHEEL

Inner ring: HAPPY, SAD, DISGUST, ANGER, FEAR, SURPRISE

Outer ring: OPTIMISTIC, PROUD, GUILTY, DEPRESSED, LONELY, DISAPPROVAL, AWFUL, DISAPPOINTED, AGGRESSIVE, MAD, HURT, SCARED, HUMILIATED, INSECURE, AMAZED, EXCITED, CONFUSED, PEACEFUL

QUALITY AND INTENSITY

FOCUS AND BREATHING	1 — 2 — 3 — 4 — 5 — 6 — 7 — 8 — 9 — 10
VISIONS AND EMOTIONS	

REFLECTIONS

🙏 I am grateful for ...

⛰️ I will accomplish ...

⚙️ I need to work on ...

📅 DATE	🕐 TIME
📍 LOCATION	⏱️ DURATION
🧘 METHOD	✱ MANTRA

MEDITATION POSITION

☐ ☐ ☐ ☐ ☐

MEDITATION FOCUS

MOOD WHEEL

THOUGHTS & INSIGHTS

QUALITY AND INTENSITY

FOCUS AND BREATHING   1 — 2 — 3 — 4 — 5 — 6 — 7 — 8 — 9 — 10
VISIONS AND EMOTIONS

REFLECTIONS

I am grateful for …

I will accomplish …

I need to work on …

📅 DATE	🕐 TIME
📍 LOCATION	⏱ DURATION
🧘 METHOD	❋ MANTRA

MEDITATION POSITION

🧘	🪑	🧍	🛌	🤸
☐	☐	☐	☐	☐

MEDITATION FOCUS

MOOD WHEEL

Mood wheel with emotions: HAPPY, SAD, DISGUST, ANGER, FEAR, SURPRISE (inner ring); OPTIMISTIC, PROUD, GUILTY, DEPRESSED, LONELY, DISAPPROVAL, AWFUL, DISAPPOINTED, AGGRESSIVE, MAD, HURT, SCARED, HUMILIATED, INSECURE, AMAZED, EXCITED, CONFUSED, PEACEFUL (outer ring).

THOUGHTS & INSIGHTS

QUALITY AND INTENSITY

	1	2	3	4	5	6	7	8	9	10
FOCUS AND BREATHING	○	○	○	○	○	○	○	○	○	○
VISIONS AND EMOTIONS	○	○	○	○	○	○	○	○	○	○

REFLECTIONS

👐 I am grateful for …

⛰ I will accomplish …

📈 I need to work on …

	DATE		TIME
	LOCATION		DURATION
	METHOD		MANTRA

MEDITATION POSITION

☐	☐	☐	☐	☐

MEDITATION FOCUS

MOOD WHEEL

Mood wheel with inner emotions: HAPPY, SAD, DISGUST, ANGER, FEAR, SURPRISE
Outer emotions: OPTIMISTIC, PROUD, GUILTY, DEPRESSED, LONELY, DISAPPROVAL, AWFUL, DISAPPOINTED, AGGRESSIVE, MAD, HURT, SCARED, HUMILIATED, INSECURE, AMAZED, EXCITED, CONFUSED, PEACEFUL

THOUGHTS & INSIGHTS

QUALITY AND INTENSITY

FOCUS AND BREATHING — 1 — 2 — 3 — 4 — 5 — 6 — 7 — 8 — 9 — 10

VISIONS AND EMOTIONS

REFLECTIONS

I am grateful for …

I will accomplish …

I need to work on …

📅 DATE	🕐 TIME
📍 LOCATION	⏱️ DURATION
🧘 METHOD	❀ MANTRA

MEDITATION POSITION

🧘 ☐	🪑 ☐	🧍 ☐	🛌 ☐	🤸 ☐

MEDITATION FOCUS

THOUGHTS & INSIGHTS

MOOD WHEEL

Mood wheel with inner emotions: HAPPY, SAD, DISGUST, ANGER, FEAR, SURPRISE; middle ring: OPTIMISTIC, PROUD, GUILTY, DEPRESSED, LONELY, DISAPPROVAL, AWFUL, DISAPPOINTED, AGGRESSIVE, MAD, HURT, SCARED, HUMILIATED, INSECURE, AMAZED, EXCITED, CONFUSED, PEACEFUL.

QUALITY AND INTENSITY

👤 FOCUS AND BREATHING	○—○—○—○—○—○—○—○—○—○
	1 — 2 — 3 — 4 — 5 — 6 — 7 — 8 — 9 — 10
👁 VISIONS AND EMOTIONS	○—○—○—○—○—○—○—○—○—○

REFLECTIONS

🙏	I am grateful for ...
⛰️	I will accomplish ...
⚙️	I need to work on ...

📅 DATE	🕐 TIME
📍 LOCATION	⏱️ DURATION
🧘 METHOD	❊ MANTRA

MEDITATION POSITION

☐ ☐ ☐ ☐ ☐

MEDITATION FOCUS

MOOD WHEEL

Mood Wheel:
- HAPPY: PEACEFUL, OPTIMISTIC, PROUD
- SAD: GUILTY, DEPRESSED, LONELY
- DISGUST: DISAPPROVAL, AWFUL, DISAPPOINTED
- ANGER: AGGRESSIVE, MAD, HURT
- FEAR: SCARED, HUMILIATED, INSECURE
- SURPRISE: AMAZED, EXCITED, CONFUSED

THOUGHTS & INSIGHTS

QUALITY AND INTENSITY

FOCUS AND BREATHING — 1 — 2 — 3 — 4 — 5 — 6 — 7 — 8 — 9 — 10

VISIONS AND EMOTIONS — 1 — 2 — 3 — 4 — 5 — 6 — 7 — 8 — 9 — 10

REFLECTIONS

🙏 I am grateful for …

⛰️ I will accomplish …

📈 I need to work on …

	DATE		TIME
	LOCATION		DURATION
	METHOD		MANTRA

MEDITATION POSITION

☐ ☐ ☐ ☐ ☐

MEDITATION FOCUS

MOOD WHEEL

Mood wheel with inner emotions: HAPPY, SURPRISE, SAD, DISGUST, FEAR, ANGER. Outer emotions: OPTIMISTIC, PROUD, GUILTY, DEPRESSED, PEACEFUL, LONELY, CONFUSED, DISAPPROVAL, EXCITED, AWFUL, AMAZED, DISAPPOINTED, INSECURE, AGGRESSIVE, HUMILIATED, MAD, SCARED, HURT.

THOUGHTS & INSIGHTS

QUALITY AND INTENSITY

FOCUS AND BREATHING

1 — 2 — 3 — 4 — 5 — 6 — 7 — 8 — 9 — 10

VISIONS AND EMOTIONS

REFLECTIONS

I am grateful for ...

I will accomplish ...

I need to work on ...

📅 DATE	🕐 TIME
📍 LOCATION	⏱️ DURATION
🧘 METHOD	✸ MANTRA

MEDITATION POSITION

🧘 ☐   🪑 ☐   🚶 ☐   🛌 ☐   🤸 ☐

MEDITATION FOCUS

MOOD WHEEL

(HAPPY: optimistic, peaceful, confused, excited, amazed; SURPRISE; FEAR: insecure, humiliated, scared; ANGER: mad, hurt, aggressive; DISGUST: disappointed, awful, disapproval; SAD: proud, guilty, depressed, lonely)

THOUGHTS & INSIGHTS

QUALITY AND INTENSITY

FOCUS AND BREATHING   1 — 2 — 3 — 4 — 5 — 6 — 7 — 8 — 9 — 10

VISIONS AND EMOTIONS   1 — 2 — 3 — 4 — 5 — 6 — 7 — 8 — 9 — 10

REFLECTIONS

🙏 I am grateful for …

⛰️ I will accomplish …

📈 I need to work on …

📅 DATE	🕐 TIME
📍 LOCATION	⏱️ DURATION
🧘 METHOD	✳️ MANTRA

MEDITATION POSITION

☐ ☐ ☐ ☐ ☐

MEDITATION FOCUS

MOOD WHEEL

Mood wheel with inner emotions: HAPPY, SAD, DISGUST, ANGER, FEAR, SURPRISE; outer emotions: OPTIMISTIC, PROUD, GUILTY, DEPRESSED, LONELY, DISAPPROVAL, AWFUL, DISAPPOINTED, AGGRESSIVE, MAD, HURT, SCARED, HUMILIATED, INSECURE, AMAZED, EXCITED, CONFUSED, PEACEFUL

THOUGHTS & INSIGHTS

QUALITY AND INTENSITY

FOCUS AND BREATHING — 1 — 2 — 3 — 4 — 5 — 6 — 7 — 8 — 9 — 10

VISIONS AND EMOTIONS

REFLECTIONS

🙏 I am grateful for …

⛰️ I will accomplish …

⚙️ I need to work on …

📅 DATE	🕐 TIME
📍 LOCATION	⏱️ DURATION
🧘 METHOD	❋ MANTRA

MEDITATION POSITION

☐ ☐ ☐ ☐ ☐

MEDITATION FOCUS

MOOD WHEEL

THOUGHTS & INSIGHTS

QUALITY AND INTENSITY

FOCUS AND BREATHING — 1 — 2 — 3 — 4 — 5 — 6 — 7 — 8 — 9 — 10

VISIONS AND EMOTIONS

REFLECTIONS

I am grateful for …

I will accomplish …

I need to work on …

DATE	TIME
LOCATION	DURATION
METHOD	MANTRA

MEDITATION POSITION

☐   ☐   ☐   ☐   ☐

MEDITATION FOCUS

THOUGHTS & INSIGHTS

MOOD WHEEL

Inner ring: HAPPY, SAD, DISGUST, ANGER, FEAR, SURPRISE

Middle ring: OPTIMISTIC, PROUD, GUILTY, DEPRESSED, LONELY, DISAPPROVAL, AWFUL, DISAPPOINTED, AGGRESSIVE, MAD, HURT, SCARED, HUMILIATED, INSECURE, AMAZED, EXCITED, CONFUSED, PEACEFUL

QUALITY AND INTENSITY

FOCUS AND BREATHING — 1 — 2 — 3 — 4 — 5 — 6 — 7 — 8 — 9 — 10

VISIONS AND EMOTIONS — 1 — 2 — 3 — 4 — 5 — 6 — 7 — 8 — 9 — 10

REFLECTIONS

I am grateful for …

I will accomplish …

I need to work on …

📅 DATE	🕐 TIME
📍 LOCATION	⏱️ DURATION
🧘 METHOD	✺ MANTRA

MEDITATION POSITION

| 🧘 ☐ | 🪑 ☐ | 🧍 ☐ | 🛌 ☐ | 🤸 ☐ |

MEDITATION FOCUS

MOOD WHEEL

(Mood wheel with inner emotions: HAPPY, SAD, SURPRISE, DISGUST, FEAR, ANGER; outer emotions: OPTIMISTIC, PROUD, GUILTY, DEPRESSED, LONELY, DISAPPROVAL, AWFUL, DISAPPOINTED, AGGRESSIVE, MAD, HURT, SCARED, HUMILIATED, INSECURE, AMAZED, EXCITED, CONFUSED, PEACEFUL)

THOUGHTS & INSIGHTS

QUALITY AND INTENSITY

FOCUS AND BREATHING — 1 — 2 — 3 — 4 — 5 — 6 — 7 — 8 — 9 — 10

VISIONS AND EMOTIONS — 1 — 2 — 3 — 4 — 5 — 6 — 7 — 8 — 9 — 10

REFLECTIONS

👏 I am grateful for …

⛰️ I will accomplish …

⚙️ I need to work on …

📅	DATE	🕐 TIME	
📍	LOCATION	⏱ DURATION	
🧘	METHOD	✿ MANTRA	

MEDITATION POSITION

🧘 ☐   🪑 ☐   🧍 ☐   🛌 ☐   🤸 ☐

MEDITATION FOCUS

MOOD WHEEL

Inner ring: HAPPY, SAD, DISGUST, ANGER, FEAR, SURPRISE

Middle ring: OPTIMISTIC, PROUD, GUILTY, DEPRESSED, LONELY, DISAPPROVAL, AWFUL, DISAPPOINTED, AGGRESSIVE, MAD, HURT, SCARED, HUMILIATED, INSECURE, AMAZED, EXCITED, CONFUSED, PEACEFUL

THOUGHTS & INSIGHTS

QUALITY AND INTENSITY

FOCUS AND BREATHING   1 — 2 — 3 — 4 — 5 — 6 — 7 — 8 — 9 — 10

VISIONS AND EMOTIONS   1 — 2 — 3 — 4 — 5 — 6 — 7 — 8 — 9 — 10

REFLECTIONS

🙏 I am grateful for ...

⛰ I will accomplish ...

⚙ I need to work on ...

DATE	TIME
LOCATION	DURATION
METHOD	MANTRA

MEDITATION POSITION

☐   ☐   ☐   ☐   ☐

MEDITATION FOCUS

MOOD WHEEL

Mood wheel with emotions: HAPPY, SAD, DISGUST, ANGER, FEAR, SURPRISE at center. Outer ring: OPTIMISTIC, PROUD, GUILTY, DEPRESSED, LONELY, DISAPPROVAL, AWFUL, DISAPPOINTED, AGGRESSIVE, MAD, HURT, SCARED, HUMILIATED, INSECURE, AMAZED, EXCITED, CONFUSED, PEACEFUL

THOUGHTS & INSIGHTS

QUALITY AND INTENSITY

FOCUS AND BREATHING — 1 — 2 — 3 — 4 — 5 — 6 — 7 — 8 — 9 — 10

VISIONS AND EMOTIONS — 1 — 2 — 3 — 4 — 5 — 6 — 7 — 8 — 9 — 10

REFLECTIONS

I am grateful for …

I will accomplish …

I need to work on …

📅	DATE	🕐	TIME
📍	LOCATION	⏱️	DURATION
🧘	METHOD	❀	MANTRA

MEDITATION POSITION

☐ ☐ ☐ ☐ ☐

MEDITATION FOCUS

MOOD WHEEL

Mood wheel with: HAPPY, SAD, SURPRISE, DISGUST, FEAR, ANGER in center. Outer emotions: OPTIMISTIC, PROUD, GUILTY, DEPRESSED, LONELY, DISAPPROVAL, AWFUL, DISAPPOINTED, AGGRESSIVE, MAD, HURT, SCARED, HUMILIATED, INSECURE, AMAZED, EXCITED, CONFUSED, PEACEFUL.

THOUGHTS & INSIGHTS

QUALITY AND INTENSITY

FOCUS AND BREATHING — 1 — 2 — 3 — 4 — 5 — 6 — 7 — 8 — 9 — 10

VISIONS AND EMOTIONS

REFLECTIONS

I am grateful for ...

I will accomplish ...

I need to work on ...

📅 DATE	🕐 TIME
📍 LOCATION	⏱ DURATION
🧘 METHOD	❄ MANTRA

MEDITATION POSITION

☐ ☐ ☐ ☐ ☐

MEDITATION FOCUS

MOOD WHEEL

Outer ring: OPTIMISTIC, PROUD, GUILTY, DEPRESSED, LONELY, DISAPPROVAL, AWFUL, DISAPPOINTED, AGGRESSIVE, MAD, HURT, SCARED, HUMILIATED, INSECURE, AMAZED, EXCITED, CONFUSED, PEACEFUL

Inner: HAPPY, SAD, DISGUST, ANGER, FEAR, SURPRISE

THOUGHTS & INSIGHTS

QUALITY AND INTENSITY

FOCUS AND BREATHING — 1 2 3 4 5 6 7 8 9 10
VISIONS AND EMOTIONS — 1 2 3 4 5 6 7 8 9 10

REFLECTIONS

I am grateful for …

I will accomplish …

I need to work on …

📅 DATE		🕐 TIME	
📍 LOCATION		⏱️ DURATION	
🧘 METHOD		🕉️ MANTRA	

MEDITATION POSITION

🧘	🧍‍♂️ (sitting on chair)	🧍	🛌	🤸
☐	☐	☐	☐	☐

MEDITATION FOCUS

_____
_____
_____

MOOD WHEEL

Inner ring: HAPPY, SAD, DISGUST, ANGER, FEAR, SURPRISE

Outer emotions: OPTIMISTIC, PROUD, GUILTY, DEPRESSED, LONELY, DISAPPROVAL, AWFUL, DISAPPOINTED, AGGRESSIVE, MAD, HURT, SCARED, HUMILIATED, INSECURE, AMAZED, EXCITED, CONFUSED, PEACEFUL

THOUGHTS & INSIGHTS

_____
_____
_____

QUALITY AND INTENSITY

	1	2	3	4	5	6	7	8	9	10
👁️‍🗨️ FOCUS AND BREATHING	○	○	○	○	○	○	○	○	○	○
👁️ VISIONS AND EMOTIONS	○	○	○	○	○	○	○	○	○	○

REFLECTIONS

🙏 I am grateful for ...

⛰️ I will accomplish ...

⚙️ I need to work on ...

	DATE		TIME
	LOCATION		DURATION
	METHOD		MANTRA

MEDITATION POSITION

☐	☐	☐	☐	☐

MEDITATION FOCUS

MOOD WHEEL

Mood wheel with core emotions: HAPPY, SAD, DISGUST, ANGER, FEAR, SURPRISE. Surrounding labels: OPTIMISTIC, PROUD, GUILTY, DEPRESSED, LONELY, DISAPPROVAL, AWFUL, DISAPPOINTED, AGGRESSIVE, MAD, HURT, SCARED, HUMILIATED, INSECURE, AMAZED, EXCITED, CONFUSED, PEACEFUL.

THOUGHTS & INSIGHTS

QUALITY AND INTENSITY

FOCUS AND BREATHING — 1 — 2 — 3 — 4 — 5 — 6 — 7 — 8 — 9 — 10

VISIONS AND EMOTIONS

REFLECTIONS

I am grateful for …

I will accomplish …

I need to work on …

	DATE		TIME
	LOCATION		DURATION
	METHOD		MANTRA

MEDITATION POSITION

☐ ☐ ☐ ☐ ☐

MEDITATION FOCUS

MOOD WHEEL

Mood wheel with emotions: HAPPY, SAD, DISGUST, ANGER, FEAR, SURPRISE in the center, surrounded by: OPTIMISTIC, PROUD, GUILTY, DEPRESSED, LONELY, DISAPPROVAL, AWFUL, DISAPPOINTED, AGGRESSIVE, MAD, HURT, SCARED, HUMILIATED, INSECURE, AMAZED, EXCITED, CONFUSED, PEACEFUL

THOUGHTS & INSIGHTS

QUALITY AND INTENSITY

FOCUS AND BREATHING — 1 — 2 — 3 — 4 — 5 — 6 — 7 — 8 — 9 — 10

VISIONS AND EMOTIONS

REFLECTIONS

I am grateful for ...

I will accomplish ...

I need to work on ...

📅 DATE	🕐 TIME
📍 LOCATION	⏱️ DURATION
🧘 METHOD	✸ MANTRA

MEDITATION POSITION

☐   ☐   ☐   ☐   ☐

MEDITATION FOCUS

MOOD WHEEL

THOUGHTS & INSIGHTS

QUALITY AND INTENSITY

FOCUS AND BREATHING — 1 — 2 — 3 — 4 — 5 — 6 — 7 — 8 — 9 — 10

VISIONS AND EMOTIONS

REFLECTIONS

I am grateful for …

I will accomplish …

I need to work on …

📅 DATE	🕐 TIME
📍 LOCATION	⏱ DURATION
🧘 METHOD	✳ MANTRA

MEDITATION POSITION

☐ ☐ ☐ ☐ ☐

MEDITATION FOCUS

MOOD WHEEL

Inner ring: HAPPY, SAD, DISGUST, ANGER, FEAR, SURPRISE

Middle ring: OPTIMISTIC, PROUD, GUILTY, DEPRESSED, LONELY, DISAPPROVAL, AWFUL, DISAPPOINTED, AGGRESSIVE, MAD, HURT, SCARED, HUMILIATED, INSECURE, AMAZED, EXCITED, CONFUSED, PEACEFUL

THOUGHTS & INSIGHTS

QUALITY AND INTENSITY

FOCUS AND BREATHING — 1 — 2 — 3 — 4 — 5 — 6 — 7 — 8 — 9 — 10

VISIONS AND EMOTIONS

REFLECTIONS

🙏 I am grateful for …

⛰ I will accomplish …

⚙ I need to work on …

📅 DATE	🕐 TIME
📍 LOCATION	⏱️ DURATION
🧘 METHOD	❂ MANTRA

MEDITATION POSITION

☐   ☐   ☐   ☐   ☐

MEDITATION FOCUS

MOOD WHEEL

HAPPY, SAD, SURPRISE, DISGUST, FEAR, ANGER
OPTIMISTIC, PROUD, GUILTY, DEPRESSED, PEACEFUL, LONELY, CONFUSED, DISAPPROVAL, EXCITED, AWFUL, AMAZED, DISAPPOINTED, INSECURE, AGGRESSIVE, HUMILIATED, MAD, SCARED, HURT

THOUGHTS & INSIGHTS

QUALITY AND INTENSITY

FOCUS AND BREATHING   1 — 2 — 3 — 4 — 5 — 6 — 7 — 8 — 9 — 10

VISIONS AND EMOTIONS

REFLECTIONS

🙏 I am grateful for …

🏔️ I will accomplish …

⚙️ I need to work on …

📅 DATE	🕐 TIME
📍 LOCATION	⏱️ DURATION
🧘 METHOD	✱ MANTRA

MEDITATION POSITION

🧘 ☐	🧎 ☐	🧍 ☐	🛌 ☐	🤸 ☐

MEDITATION FOCUS

THOUGHTS & INSIGHTS

MOOD WHEEL

Mood wheel with inner emotions: HAPPY, SAD, SURPRISE, DISGUST, FEAR, ANGER; outer emotions: OPTIMISTIC, PROUD, GUILTY, DEPRESSED, PEACEFUL, LONELY, CONFUSED, DISAPPROVAL, EXCITED, AWFUL, AMAZED, DISAPPOINTED, INSECURE, AGGRESSIVE, HUMILIATED, SCARED, HURT, MAD

QUALITY AND INTENSITY

FOCUS AND BREATHING	1 — 2 — 3 — 4 — 5 — 6 — 7 — 8 — 9 — 10
VISIONS AND EMOTIONS	1 — 2 — 3 — 4 — 5 — 6 — 7 — 8 — 9 — 10

REFLECTIONS

🙏 I am grateful for ...

⛰️ I will accomplish ...

📊 I need to work on ...

📅 DATE	🕐 TIME
📍 LOCATION	⏱️ DURATION
🧘 METHOD	❁ MANTRA

MEDITATION POSITION

☐ ☐ ☐ ☐ ☐

MEDITATION FOCUS

MOOD WHEEL

- HAPPY: OPTIMISTIC, PEACEFUL, PROUD
- SAD: GUILTY, DEPRESSED, LONELY
- DISGUST: DISAPPROVAL, AWFUL, DISAPPOINTED
- ANGER: AGGRESSIVE, MAD, HURT
- FEAR: SCARED, HUMILIATED, INSECURE
- SURPRISE: AMAZED, EXCITED, CONFUSED

THOUGHTS & INSIGHTS

QUALITY AND INTENSITY

FOCUS AND BREATHING — 1 — 2 — 3 — 4 — 5 — 6 — 7 — 8 — 9 — 10

VISIONS AND EMOTIONS — 1 — 2 — 3 — 4 — 5 — 6 — 7 — 8 — 9 — 10

REFLECTIONS

🙏 I am grateful for …

⛰️ I will accomplish …

⚙️ I need to work on …

📅 DATE	🕐 TIME
📍 LOCATION	⏱ DURATION
🧘 METHOD	✻ MANTRA

MEDITATION POSITION

☐ 　 ☐ 　 ☐ 　 ☐ 　 ☐

MEDITATION FOCUS

MOOD WHEEL

THOUGHTS & INSIGHTS

QUALITY AND INTENSITY

- FOCUS AND BREATHING
- VISIONS AND EMOTIONS

1 — 2 — 3 — 4 — 5 — 6 — 7 — 8 — 9 — 10

REFLECTIONS

- I am grateful for …
- I will accomplish …
- I need to work on …

DATE	TIME
LOCATION	DURATION
METHOD	MANTRA

MEDITATION POSITION

☐ ☐ ☐ ☐ ☐

MEDITATION FOCUS

MOOD WHEEL

- HAPPY (OPTIMISTIC, PROUD, PEACEFUL)
- SAD (GUILTY, DEPRESSED, LONELY)
- SURPRISE (CONFUSED, EXCITED, AMAZED)
- DISGUST (DISAPPROVAL, AWFUL, DISAPPOINTED)
- FEAR (INSECURE, HUMILIATED, SCARED)
- ANGER (HURT, MAD, AGGRESSIVE)

THOUGHTS & INSIGHTS

QUALITY AND INTENSITY

FOCUS AND BREATHING — 1 — 2 — 3 — 4 — 5 — 6 — 7 — 8 — 9 — 10

VISIONS AND EMOTIONS — 1 — 2 — 3 — 4 — 5 — 6 — 7 — 8 — 9 — 10

REFLECTIONS

I am grateful for …

I will accomplish …

I need to work on …

📅 DATE	🕐 TIME
📍 LOCATION	⏱ DURATION
🧘 METHOD	❋ MANTRA

MEDITATION POSITION

☐ ☐ ☐ ☐ ☐

MEDITATION FOCUS

THOUGHTS & INSIGHTS

MOOD WHEEL

Happy, Sad, Disgust, Anger, Fear, Surprise
Optimistic, Proud, Guilty, Depressed, Lonely, Disapproval, Awful, Disappointed, Aggressive, Mad, Hurt, Scared, Humiliated, Insecure, Amazed, Excited, Confused, Peaceful

QUALITY AND INTENSITY

FOCUS AND BREATHING — 1 — 2 — 3 — 4 — 5 — 6 — 7 — 8 — 9 — 10

VISIONS AND EMOTIONS — 1 — 2 — 3 — 4 — 5 — 6 — 7 — 8 — 9 — 10

REFLECTIONS

🙏 I am grateful for …

⛰ I will accomplish …

⚙ I need to work on …

DATE	TIME
LOCATION	DURATION
METHOD	MANTRA

MEDITATION POSITION

☐   ☐   ☐   ☐   ☐

MEDITATION FOCUS

MOOD WHEEL

Happy: OPTIMISTIC, PROUD, PEACEFUL
Sad: GUILTY, DEPRESSED, LONELY
Disgust: DISAPPROVAL, AWFUL, DISAPPOINTED
Anger: AGGRESSIVE, MAD, HURT
Fear: SCARED, HUMILIATED, INSECURE
Surprise: AMAZED, EXCITED, CONFUSED

THOUGHTS & INSIGHTS

QUALITY AND INTENSITY

FOCUS AND BREATHING — 1 – 2 – 3 – 4 – 5 – 6 – 7 – 8 – 9 – 10

VISIONS AND EMOTIONS — 1 – 2 – 3 – 4 – 5 – 6 – 7 – 8 – 9 – 10

REFLECTIONS

I am grateful for ...

I will accomplish ...

I need to work on ...

📅 DATE	🕐 TIME
📍 LOCATION	⏱ DURATION
🧘 METHOD	✺ MANTRA

MEDITATION POSITION

🧘 ☐	🪑 ☐	🧍 ☐	🛌 ☐	🤸 ☐

MEDITATION FOCUS

THOUGHTS & INSIGHTS

MOOD WHEEL

Mood wheel with inner emotions: HAPPY, SAD, SURPRISE, DISGUST, FEAR, ANGER; and outer emotions: PROUD, GUILTY, DEPRESSED, LONELY, DISAPPROVAL, AWFUL, DISAPPOINTED, AGGRESSIVE, MAD, HURT, SCARED, HUMILIATED, INSECURE, AMAZED, EXCITED, CONFUSED, PEACEFUL, OPTIMISTIC.

QUALITY AND INTENSITY

	1	2	3	4	5	6	7	8	9	10
FOCUS AND BREATHING	○	○	○	○	○	○	○	○	○	○
VISIONS AND EMOTIONS	○	○	○	○	○	○	○	○	○	○

REFLECTIONS

🙏 I am grateful for …

⛰ I will accomplish …

⚙ I need to work on …

DATE	TIME
LOCATION	DURATION
METHOD	MANTRA

MEDITATION POSITION

☐ ☐ ☐ ☐ ☐

MEDITATION FOCUS

MOOD WHEEL

Mood wheel with emotions: HAPPY, SAD, DISGUST, ANGER, FEAR, SURPRISE at center; outer ring: OPTIMISTIC, PROUD, GUILTY, DEPRESSED, LONELY, DISAPPROVAL, AWFUL, DISAPPOINTED, AGGRESSIVE, MAD, HURT, SCARED, HUMILIATED, INSECURE, AMAZED, EXCITED, CONFUSED, PEACEFUL

THOUGHTS & INSIGHTS

QUALITY AND INTENSITY

FOCUS AND BREATHING — 1 — 2 — 3 — 4 — 5 — 6 — 7 — 8 — 9 — 10

VISIONS AND EMOTIONS

REFLECTIONS

I am grateful for …

I will accomplish …

I need to work on …

	DATE		TIME
	LOCATION		DURATION
	METHOD		MANTRA

MEDITATION POSITION

☐   ☐   ☐   ☐   ☐

MEDITATION FOCUS

MOOD WHEEL

Mood wheel with inner emotions: HAPPY, SAD, DISGUST, ANGER, FEAR, SURPRISE. Outer emotions: OPTIMISTIC, PROUD, GUILTY, DEPRESSED, LONELY, DISAPPROVAL, AWFUL, DISAPPOINTED, AGGRESSIVE, MAD, HURT, SCARED, HUMILIATED, INSECURE, AMAZED, EXCITED, CONFUSED, PEACEFUL.

THOUGHTS & INSIGHTS

QUALITY AND INTENSITY

FOCUS AND BREATHING — 1 — 2 — 3 — 4 — 5 — 6 — 7 — 8 — 9 — 10

VISIONS AND EMOTIONS

REFLECTIONS

I am grateful for ...

I will accomplish ...

I need to work on ...

DATE	TIME
LOCATION	DURATION
METHOD	MANTRA

MEDITATION POSITION

☐ ☐ ☐ ☐ ☐

MEDITATION FOCUS

MOOD WHEEL

Mood wheel segments: HAPPY (OPTIMISTIC, PEACEFUL, PROUD), SAD (GUILTY, DEPRESSED, LONELY), DISGUST (DISAPPROVAL, AWFUL, DISAPPOINTED), ANGER (AGGRESSIVE, MAD, HURT), FEAR (SCARED, HUMILIATED, INSECURE), SURPRISE (AMAZED, EXCITED, CONFUSED)

THOUGHTS & INSIGHTS

QUALITY AND INTENSITY

FOCUS AND BREATHING — 1 2 3 4 5 6 7 8 9 10

VISIONS AND EMOTIONS — 1 2 3 4 5 6 7 8 9 10

REFLECTIONS

I am grateful for …

I will accomplish …

I need to work on …

📅 DATE	🕐 TIME
📍 LOCATION	⏱ DURATION
🧘 METHOD	❁ MANTRA

MEDITATION POSITION

☐ ☐ ☐ ☐ ☐

MEDITATION FOCUS

MOOD WHEEL

Inner ring: HAPPY, SAD, DISGUST, ANGER, FEAR, SURPRISE

Outer labels: OPTIMISTIC, PROUD, GUILTY, DEPRESSED, LONELY, DISAPPROVAL, AWFUL, DISAPPOINTED, AGGRESSIVE, MAD, HURT, SCARED, HUMILIATED, INSECURE, AMAZED, EXCITED, CONFUSED, PEACEFUL

THOUGHTS & INSIGHTS

QUALITY AND INTENSITY

FOCUS AND BREATHING — 1 — 2 — 3 — 4 — 5 — 6 — 7 — 8 — 9 — 10

VISIONS AND EMOTIONS

REFLECTIONS

🙏 I am grateful for …

⛰ I will accomplish …

⚙ I need to work on …

📅 DATE	🕐 TIME
📍 LOCATION	⏱️ DURATION
🧘 METHOD	❄️ MANTRA

MEDITATION POSITION

☐ 🧘 ☐ 🪑 ☐ 🧍 ☐ 🛌 ☐ 🤸

MEDITATION FOCUS

MOOD WHEEL

(Mood wheel with inner categories: HAPPY, SAD, SURPRISE, DISGUST, FEAR, ANGER; outer emotions: OPTIMISTIC, PROUD, GUILTY, DEPRESSED, LONELY, DISAPPROVAL, AWFUL, DISAPPOINTED, AGGRESSIVE, MAD, HURT, SCARED, HUMILIATED, INSECURE, AMAZED, EXCITED, CONFUSED, PEACEFUL)

THOUGHTS & INSIGHTS

QUALITY AND INTENSITY

	1 — 2 — 3 — 4 — 5 — 6 — 7 — 8 — 9 — 10
FOCUS AND BREATHING	○ ○ ○ ○ ○ ○ ○ ○ ○ ○
VISIONS AND EMOTIONS	○ ○ ○ ○ ○ ○ ○ ○ ○ ○

REFLECTIONS

🙏 I am grateful for …

⛰️ I will accomplish …

📈 I need to work on …

📅 DATE	🕐 TIME
📍 LOCATION	⏱️ DURATION
🧘 METHOD	✴️ MANTRA

MEDITATION POSITION

☐ ☐ ☐ ☐ ☐

MEDITATION FOCUS

MOOD WHEEL

Mood wheel with emotions: HAPPY (optimistic, proud, peaceful), SAD (guilty, depressed, lonely), DISGUST (disapproval, awful, disappointed), ANGER (aggressive, mad, hurt), FEAR (scared, humiliated, insecure), SURPRISE (amazed, excited, confused)

THOUGHTS & INSIGHTS

QUALITY AND INTENSITY

FOCUS AND BREATHING — 1 — 2 — 3 — 4 — 5 — 6 — 7 — 8 — 9 — 10

VISIONS AND EMOTIONS — 1 — 2 — 3 — 4 — 5 — 6 — 7 — 8 — 9 — 10

REFLECTIONS

👐 I am grateful for …

⛰️ I will accomplish …

📈 I need to work on …

📅 DATE	🕐 TIME
📍 LOCATION	⏱️ DURATION
🧘 METHOD	❁ MANTRA

MEDITATION POSITION

☐   ☐   ☐   ☐   ☐

MEDITATION FOCUS

MOOD WHEEL

(Mood wheel with inner ring: HAPPY, SAD, DISGUST, ANGER, FEAR, SURPRISE; outer ring: OPTIMISTIC, PROUD, GUILTY, DEPRESSED, LONELY, DISAPPROVAL, AWFUL, DISAPPOINTED, AGGRESSIVE, MAD, HURT, SCARED, HUMILIATED, INSECURE, AMAZED, EXCITED, CONFUSED, PEACEFUL)

THOUGHTS & INSIGHTS

QUALITY AND INTENSITY

FOCUS AND BREATHING   1 — 2 — 3 — 4 — 5 — 6 — 7 — 8 — 9 — 10
VISIONS AND EMOTIONS

REFLECTIONS

I am grateful for …

I will accomplish …

I need to work on …

📅 DATE	🕐 TIME
📍 LOCATION	⏱️ DURATION
🧘 METHOD	❀ MANTRA

MEDITATION POSITION

☐   ☐   ☐   ☐   ☐

MEDITATION FOCUS

MOOD WHEEL

Inner ring: HAPPY, SAD, DISGUST, ANGER, FEAR, SURPRISE

Middle ring: OPTIMISTIC, PROUD, GUILTY, DEPRESSED, LONELY, DISAPPROVAL, AWFUL, DISAPPOINTED, AGGRESSIVE, MAD, HURT, SCARED, HUMILIATED, INSECURE, AMAZED, EXCITED, CONFUSED, PEACEFUL

THOUGHTS & INSIGHTS

QUALITY AND INTENSITY

	1	2	3	4	5	6	7	8	9	10
FOCUS AND BREATHING	○	○	○	○	○	○	○	○	○	○
VISIONS AND EMOTIONS	○	○	○	○	○	○	○	○	○	○

REFLECTIONS

🙏 I am grateful for …

⛰️ I will accomplish …

⚙️ I need to work on …

DATE	TIME
LOCATION	DURATION
METHOD	MANTRA

MEDITATION POSITION

☐ ☐ ☐ ☐ ☐

MEDITATION FOCUS

MOOD WHEEL

Outer ring: OPTIMISTIC, PROUD, GUILTY, DEPRESSED, LONELY, DISAPPROVAL, AWFUL, DISAPPOINTED, AGGRESSIVE, MAD, HURT, SCARED, HUMILIATED, INSECURE, AMAZED, EXCITED, CONFUSED, PEACEFUL

Inner ring: HAPPY, SAD, DISGUST, ANGER, FEAR, SURPRISE

THOUGHTS & INSIGHTS

QUALITY AND INTENSITY

FOCUS AND BREATHING — 1 — 2 — 3 — 4 — 5 — 6 — 7 — 8 — 9 — 10

VISIONS AND EMOTIONS

REFLECTIONS

I am grateful for ...

I will accomplish ...

I need to work on ...

📅 DATE	🕐 TIME
📍 LOCATION	⏱ DURATION
🧘 METHOD	✻ MANTRA

MEDITATION POSITION

☐ ☐ ☐ ☐ ☐

MEDITATION FOCUS

MOOD WHEEL

Mood wheel with core emotions: HAPPY, SURPRISE, SAD, DISGUST, FEAR, ANGER. Surrounding emotions include: OPTIMISTIC, PROUD, GUILTY, DEPRESSED, PEACEFUL, LONELY, CONFUSED, DISAPPROVAL, EXCITED, AWFUL, AMAZED, DISAPPOINTED, INSECURE, AGGRESSIVE, HUMILIATED, SCARED, HURT, MAD.

THOUGHTS & INSIGHTS

QUALITY AND INTENSITY

FOCUS AND BREATHING — 1 — 2 — 3 — 4 — 5 — 6 — 7 — 8 — 9 — 10

VISIONS AND EMOTIONS

REFLECTIONS

I am grateful for …

I will accomplish …

I need to work on …

📅 DATE	🕐 TIME
📍 LOCATION	⏱ DURATION
🧘 METHOD	❀ MANTRA

MEDITATION POSITION

☐ ☐ ☐ ☐ ☐

MEDITATION FOCUS

MOOD WHEEL

- HAPPY: OPTIMISTIC, PROUD, PEACEFUL, CONFUSED, EXCITED, AMAZED
- SAD: GUILTY, DEPRESSED, LONELY
- DISGUST: DISAPPROVAL, AWFUL, DISAPPOINTED
- ANGER: AGGRESSIVE, MAD, HURT
- FEAR: INSECURE, HUMILIATED, SCARED
- SURPRISE

THOUGHTS & INSIGHTS

QUALITY AND INTENSITY

FOCUS AND BREATHING — 1 — 2 — 3 — 4 — 5 — 6 — 7 — 8 — 9 — 10

VISIONS AND EMOTIONS — 1 — 2 — 3 — 4 — 5 — 6 — 7 — 8 — 9 — 10

REFLECTIONS

👏 I am grateful for …

⛰ I will accomplish …

⚙ I need to work on …

📅 DATE	🕐 TIME
📍 LOCATION	⏱️ DURATION
🧘 METHOD	✳️ MANTRA

MEDITATION POSITION

🧘	🪑	🧍	🛌	🤸
☐	☐	☐	☐	☐

MEDITATION FOCUS

MOOD WHEEL

Mood wheel with emotions: HAPPY (OPTIMISTIC, PROUD, PEACEFUL), SAD (GUILTY, DEPRESSED, LONELY), DISGUST (DISAPPROVAL, AWFUL, DISAPPOINTED), ANGER (AGGRESSIVE, MAD, HURT), FEAR (SCARED, HUMILIATED, INSECURE), SURPRISE (AMAZED, EXCITED, CONFUSED)

THOUGHTS & INSIGHTS

QUALITY AND INTENSITY

FOCUS AND BREATHING — 1 — 2 — 3 — 4 — 5 — 6 — 7 — 8 — 9 — 10

VISIONS AND EMOTIONS

REFLECTIONS

🙏 I am grateful for …

⛰️ I will accomplish …

⚙️ I need to work on …

DATE	TIME
LOCATION	DURATION
METHOD	MANTRA

MEDITATION POSITION

☐ ☐ ☐ ☐ ☐

MEDITATION FOCUS

MOOD WHEEL

Mood wheel emotions: HAPPY, SAD, DISGUST, ANGER, FEAR, SURPRISE
Outer: OPTIMISTIC, PROUD, GUILTY, DEPRESSED, LONELY, DISAPPROVAL, AWFUL, DISAPPOINTED, AGGRESSIVE, MAD, HURT, SCARED, HUMILIATED, INSECURE, AMAZED, EXCITED, CONFUSED, PEACEFUL

THOUGHTS & INSIGHTS

QUALITY AND INTENSITY

FOCUS AND BREATHING — 1 — 2 — 3 — 4 — 5 — 6 — 7 — 8 — 9 — 10

VISIONS AND EMOTIONS

REFLECTIONS

I am grateful for …

I will accomplish …

I need to work on …

📅 DATE	🕐 TIME
📍 LOCATION	⏱️ DURATION
🧘 METHOD	✺ MANTRA

MEDITATION POSITION

☐ ☐ ☐ ☐ ☐

MEDITATION FOCUS

MOOD WHEEL

Mood wheel with emotions: HAPPY, SAD, DISGUST, ANGER, FEAR, SURPRISE — surrounded by OPTIMISTIC, PROUD, GUILTY, DEPRESSED, LONELY, DISAPPROVAL, AWFUL, DISAPPOINTED, AGGRESSIVE, MAD, HURT, SCARED, HUMILIATED, INSECURE, AMAZED, EXCITED, CONFUSED, PEACEFUL.

THOUGHTS & INSIGHTS

QUALITY AND INTENSITY

FOCUS AND BREATHING 1 — 2 — 3 — 4 — 5 — 6 — 7 — 8 — 9 — 10
VISIONS AND EMOTIONS

REFLECTIONS

I am grateful for ...

I will accomplish ...

I need to work on ...

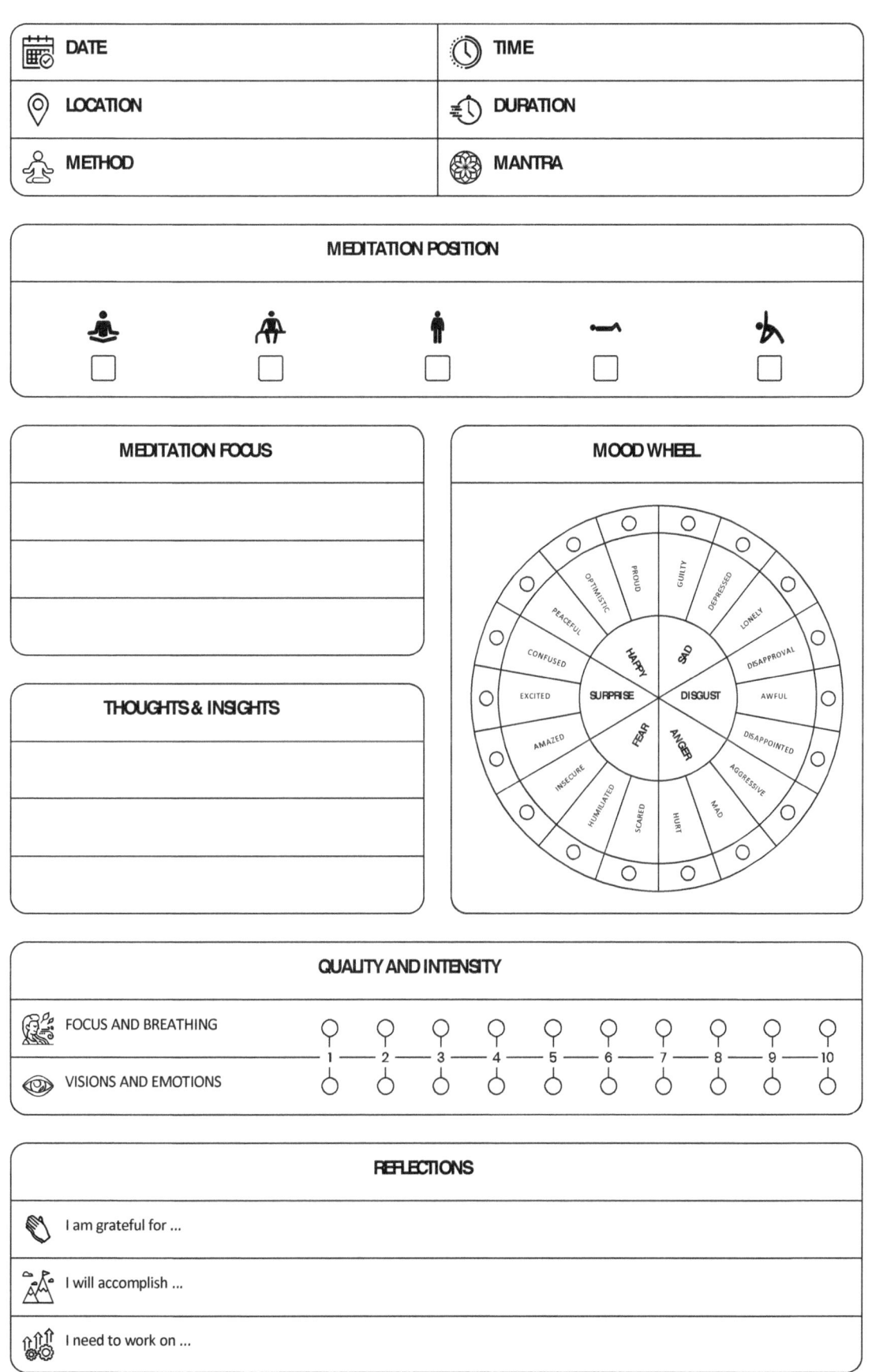

📅 DATE	🕐 TIME
📍 LOCATION	⏱️ DURATION
🧘 METHOD	❁ MANTRA

MEDITATION POSITION

🧘 ☐   🪑 ☐   🧍 ☐   🛌 ☐   🤸 ☐

MEDITATION FOCUS

MOOD WHEEL

Mood wheel with inner emotions: HAPPY, SAD, SURPRISE, DISGUST, FEAR, ANGER; outer emotions: OPTIMISTIC, PROUD, GUILTY, DEPRESSED, LONELY, DISAPPROVAL, AWFUL, DISAPPOINTED, AGGRESSIVE, MAD, HURT, SCARED, HUMILIATED, INSECURE, AMAZED, EXCITED, CONFUSED, PEACEFUL

THOUGHTS & INSIGHTS

QUALITY AND INTENSITY

FOCUS AND BREATHING   1 — 2 — 3 — 4 — 5 — 6 — 7 — 8 — 9 — 10

VISIONS AND EMOTIONS

REFLECTIONS

🙏 I am grateful for ...

⛰️ I will accomplish ...

⚙️ I need to work on ...

📅	DATE	🕐	TIME
📍	LOCATION	⏱️	DURATION
🧘	METHOD	❋	MANTRA

MEDITATION POSITION

☐   ☐   ☐   ☐   ☐

MEDITATION FOCUS

MOOD WHEEL

THOUGHTS & INSIGHTS

QUALITY AND INTENSITY

FOCUS AND BREATHING   ○—○—○—○—○—○—○—○—○—○
                     1   2   3   4   5   6   7   8   9   10
VISIONS AND EMOTIONS ○ ○ ○ ○ ○ ○ ○ ○ ○ ○

REFLECTIONS

🙏 I am grateful for …

⛰️ I will accomplish …

📈 I need to work on …

📅 DATE	🕐 TIME
📍 LOCATION	⏱️ DURATION
🧘 METHOD	❁ MANTRA

MEDITATION POSITION

🧘 ☐   🪑 ☐   🧍 ☐   🛌 ☐   🤸 ☐

MEDITATION FOCUS

MOOD WHEEL

(Mood wheel with segments: HAPPY, SAD, DISGUST, ANGER, FEAR, SURPRISE — outer labels: OPTIMISTIC, PROUD, GUILTY, DEPRESSED, LONELY, DISAPPROVAL, AWFUL, DISAPPOINTED, AGGRESSIVE, MAD, HURT, SCARED, HUMILIATED, INSECURE, AMAZED, EXCITED, CONFUSED, PEACEFUL)

THOUGHTS & INSIGHTS

QUALITY AND INTENSITY

FOCUS AND BREATHING   1 — 2 — 3 — 4 — 5 — 6 — 7 — 8 — 9 — 10

VISIONS AND EMOTIONS   1 — 2 — 3 — 4 — 5 — 6 — 7 — 8 — 9 — 10

REFLECTIONS

🙏 I am grateful for …

⛰️ I will accomplish …

⚙️ I need to work on …

📅 DATE	🕐 TIME
📍 LOCATION	⏱️ DURATION
🧘 METHOD	❂ MANTRA

MEDITATION POSITION

🧘	🪑	🧍	🛌	🤸
☐	☐	☐	☐	☐

MEDITATION FOCUS

THOUGHTS & INSIGHTS

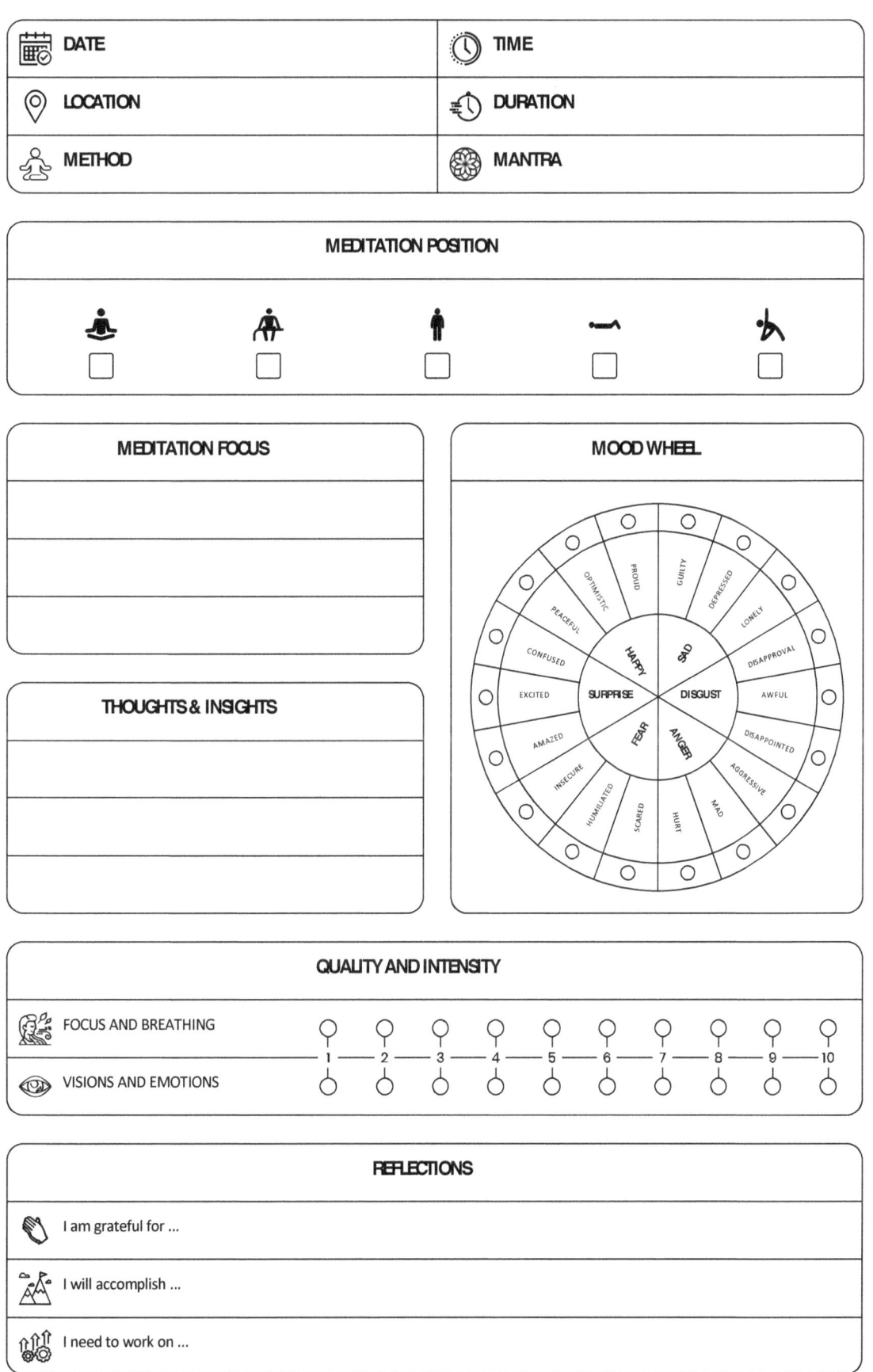

MOOD WHEEL

QUALITY AND INTENSITY

FOCUS AND BREATHING ○—○—○—○—○—○—○—○—○—○
1 — 2 — 3 — 4 — 5 — 6 — 7 — 8 — 9 — 10
VISIONS AND EMOTIONS ○ ○ ○ ○ ○ ○ ○ ○ ○ ○

REFLECTIONS

🙏 I am grateful for …

⛰️ I will accomplish …

⚙️ I need to work on …

📅 DATE		🕐 TIME	
📍 LOCATION		⏱️ DURATION	
🧘 METHOD		❂ MANTRA	

MEDITATION POSITION

🧘	🪑	🧍	🛌	🤸
☐	☐	☐	☐	☐

MEDITATION FOCUS

MOOD WHEEL

Mood wheel with emotions: HAPPY, SAD, DISGUST, ANGER, FEAR, SURPRISE — surrounded by: OPTIMISTIC, PROUD, GUILTY, DEPRESSED, LONELY, DISAPPROVAL, AWFUL, DISAPPOINTED, AGGRESSIVE, MAD, HURT, SCARED, HUMILIATED, INSECURE, AMAZED, EXCITED, CONFUSED, PEACEFUL

THOUGHTS & INSIGHTS

QUALITY AND INTENSITY

	1	2	3	4	5	6	7	8	9	10
FOCUS AND BREATHING	○	○	○	○	○	○	○	○	○	○
VISIONS AND EMOTIONS	○	○	○	○	○	○	○	○	○	○

REFLECTIONS

🙏 I am grateful for …

⛰️ I will accomplish …

⚙️ I need to work on …

DATE	TIME
LOCATION	DURATION
METHOD	MANTRA

MEDITATION POSITION

☐ ☐ ☐ ☐ ☐

MEDITATION FOCUS

MOOD WHEEL

Mood wheel with inner emotions: HAPPY, SAD, DISGUST, ANGER, FEAR, SURPRISE; outer emotions: OPTIMISTIC, PROUD, GUILTY, DEPRESSED, LONELY, DISAPPROVAL, AWFUL, DISAPPOINTED, AGGRESSIVE, MAD, HURT, SCARED, HUMILIATED, INSECURE, AMAZED, EXCITED, CONFUSED, PEACEFUL

THOUGHTS & INSIGHTS

QUALITY AND INTENSITY

| FOCUS AND BREATHING | 1 — 2 — 3 — 4 — 5 — 6 — 7 — 8 — 9 — 10 |
| VISIONS AND EMOTIONS | 1 — 2 — 3 — 4 — 5 — 6 — 7 — 8 — 9 — 10 |

REFLECTIONS

I am grateful for ...

I will accomplish ...

I need to work on ...

DATE	TIME
LOCATION	DURATION
METHOD	MANTRA

MEDITATION POSITION

☐   ☐   ☐   ☐   ☐

MEDITATION FOCUS

THOUGHTS & INSIGHTS

MOOD WHEEL

Inner ring: HAPPY, SAD, DISGUST, ANGER, FEAR, SURPRISE

Outer ring: OPTIMISTIC, PROUD, GUILTY, DEPRESSED, LONELY, DISAPPROVAL, AWFUL, DISAPPOINTED, AGGRESSIVE, MAD, HURT, SCARED, HUMILIATED, INSECURE, AMAZED, EXCITED, CONFUSED, PEACEFUL

QUALITY AND INTENSITY

| FOCUS AND BREATHING | 1 — 2 — 3 — 4 — 5 — 6 — 7 — 8 — 9 — 10 |
| VISIONS AND EMOTIONS | 1 — 2 — 3 — 4 — 5 — 6 — 7 — 8 — 9 — 10 |

REFLECTIONS

I am grateful for …

I will accomplish …

I need to work on …

📅	DATE	🕐	TIME
📍	LOCATION	⏱️	DURATION
🧘	METHOD	✾	MANTRA

MEDITATION POSITION

☐ ☐ ☐ ☐ ☐

MEDITATION FOCUS

MOOD WHEEL

Mood wheel with emotions: HAPPY, SAD, DISGUST, ANGER, FEAR, SURPRISE — including OPTIMISTIC, PROUD, GUILTY, DEPRESSED, PEACEFUL, LONELY, CONFUSED, DISAPPROVAL, EXCITED, AWFUL, AMAZED, DISAPPOINTED, INSECURE, AGGRESSIVE, HUMILIATED, MAD, SCARED, HURT.

THOUGHTS & INSIGHTS

QUALITY AND INTENSITY

FOCUS AND BREATHING — 1 — 2 — 3 — 4 — 5 — 6 — 7 — 8 — 9 — 10

VISIONS AND EMOTIONS — 1 — 2 — 3 — 4 — 5 — 6 — 7 — 8 — 9 — 10

REFLECTIONS

👏 I am grateful for …

🏔️ I will accomplish …

⚙️ I need to work on …

📅 DATE	🕐 TIME
📍 LOCATION	⏱️ DURATION
🧘 METHOD	✳️ MANTRA

MEDITATION POSITION

🧘 ☐   🪑 ☐   🧍 ☐   🛌 ☐   🤸 ☐

MEDITATION FOCUS

MOOD WHEEL

Mood Wheel: HAPPY, SAD, DISGUST, ANGER, FEAR, SURPRISE — with outer ring: OPTIMISTIC, PROUD, GUILTY, DEPRESSED, LONELY, DISAPPROVAL, AWFUL, DISAPPOINTED, AGGRESSIVE, MAD, HURT, SCARED, HUMILIATED, INSECURE, AMAZED, EXCITED, CONFUSED, PEACEFUL

THOUGHTS & INSIGHTS

QUALITY AND INTENSITY

FOCUS AND BREATHING   1 — 2 — 3 — 4 — 5 — 6 — 7 — 8 — 9 — 10

VISIONS AND EMOTIONS

REFLECTIONS

🙏 I am grateful for …

⛰️ I will accomplish …

⚙️ I need to work on …

www.ingramcontent.com/pod-product-compliance
Lightning Source LLC
Chambersburg PA
CBHW081232080526
44587CB00022B/3910